"While Mark was at Florida State to lead Mark to Christ in 1986. His life has never been the same. Mark not only talks the talk but he walks the walk. He is a great role model for young people to follow."

Bobby Bowden, former head football coach,
Florida State University

"If you love faith, family, and football, with some wonderful leadership and decision-making tools, you will love *Make the Call.*"

John Maxwell, #1 *New York Times*
bestselling author

"*Make the Call* will entertain, inspire, and also challenge you to make decisions that will bless you and others that you influence. This is a must-read!"

Jon Gordon, author of *The Energy Bus* and
The Power of Positive Leadership

"I have always had great respect and admiration for Mark Richt. Through his book *Make the Call,* we can now relive some of Coach Richt's great and not-so-great moments in his career. This book will give you great insight into the life of a Division I champion coach and man."

Dabo Swinney, national championship-winning
head football coach, Clemson University Tigers

"I have admired Mark Richt as a coach because he not only produced great teams but great young men as well. *Make the Call* will give you some of Mark's coaching secrets, but also give you the secrets to making the truly important decisions in life."

Tony Dungy, bestselling author and former head coach of the Tampa Bay Buccaneers and Indianapolis Colts

"If you want to know what made Coach Richt tick throughout his days as a coach and mentor, *Make the Call* will tell you where his strength came from."

Tony Evans, president, The Urban Alternative and senior pastor, Oak Cliff Bible Fellowship

MAKE THE CALL

MAKE THE CALL
MARK RICHT

with Lawrence Kimbrough

GAME-DAY WISDOM FOR LIFE'S DEFINING MOMENTS

B&H
PUBLISHING
NASHVILLE, TENNESSEE

978-1-0877-4186-4

Published by B&H Publishing Group
Nashville, Tennessee

Published in association with the literary agency of Legacy, LLC, 501 N. Orlando Avenue, Suite #313-348, Winter Park, FL 32789 and in association with the talent agency of CSE Talent, LLC, 150 Interstate North Parkway, Atlanta, GA 30339.

Dewey Decimal Classification: 153.8
Subject Heading: CHRISTIAN LIFE / DECISION MAKING / PROBLEM SOLVING

Main Scripture: New American Standard Bible 1995, New American Standard Bible®, Copyright © 1960, 1971, 1977, 1995 by The Lockman Foundation. All rights reserved.

Scripture references marked NKJV are taken from New King James Version®, copyright © 1982 by Thomas Nelson. Used by permission. All rights reserved.

Scripture references marked ESV are taken from English Standard Version. ESV® Text Edition: 2016. Copyright © 2001 by Crossway Bibles, a publishing ministry of Good News Publishers.

Scripture references marked HCSB are taken from Holman Christian Standard Bible, copyright © 1999, 2000, 2002, 2003, 2009 by Holman Bible Publishers, Nashville Tennessee. All rights reserved.

Scripture references marked CSB are taken from The Christian Standard Bible. Copyright © 2017 by Holman Bible Publishers. Used by permission. Christian Standard Bible®, and CSB® are federally registered trademarks of Holman Bible Publishers, all rights reserved.

Cover photo © Micah Kandros; Kara Gaylor, stylist.

Radio broadcast transcriptions on pages 118 and 127 are used with permission of the University of Georgia Athletic Association.

Press conference quotations on page 189: https://www.youtube.com/watch?v=DTt8r8qCx5A and on pages 217–222: https://www.youtube.com/watch?v=P3xmmHC1WeI.

1 2 3 4 5 6 • 25 24 23 22 21

*I dedicate this book, first and foremost,
to my Lord and Savior, Jesus Christ.*

*And to my beautiful wife, Katharyn,
who has been my rock through it all.*

Contents

Part IV: The Miami Years

Introduction

"Make the Call, Coach"

Miami hadn't beaten Florida State in seven years.

Miami, winner of five national championships. Miami, the inventors of swag. Miami, the orange-and-green gate-crasher who'd risen up out of seeming nowhere in the 1980s to shake up the blue bloods of college football. Miami, my alma mater. Miami, the U.

Miami—who was now my football team.

It was October 7, 2017. My second year as head coach in Coral Gables, and my first trip back to Tallahassee as the enemy. This was special to me. At 3:30 in the afternoon, at kickoff under bright sunlight on Bobby Bowden Field, at Doak Campbell Stadium, this was our chance to prove that the U was worthy of the nation's attention once again.

The year before, at home, we'd come close to beating them, close to at least pushing the game into overtime. Our junior placekicker, Michael Badgley, had seen his streak of made extra points end at seventy-two, with just over a minute to play. A leaping Seminole lineman had pawed the ball out of the sky, right after we'd scored late to pull the game to within one.

And this year—man, this year, it looked like they'd gotten us again. Tied at the half, tied again at the start of the fourth quarter, we finally nudged ahead 17–13 on a short touchdown pass from Malik Rosier to Braxton Berrios. But freshman Florida State quarterback James Blackman, filling in for their injured star sophomore Deondre Francois, marched his offense seventy-five yards on a four-minute scoring drive, capped by a crushing touchdown completion to a wide-open receiver in the right corner of the end zone.

New score—Florida State 20, Miami 17.

Time remaining on the clock—1:24.

The home team fans erupted. Our undefeated, thirteenth-ranked Hurricanes—winner of eight games in a row dating back to the previous year—had come into town and, from the way it was looking, we were about to get whipped for the eighth straight time. From the dancing on the other sideline, to the chanted Seminole Chops thundering down around the stadium, the mood among most of the 78,000 in attendance was clear. This ball game was over.

Only not to us.

We knew their defense, playing to preserve a win in the last minute of the game, would leave enough space underneath for us to pick up chunks of yardage, allowing us to draw closer and closer into field goal range. If we could just get to about their 35 or so. Michael hadn't missed a field goal from between 40–49 yards, not just in this season, but in his entire career. We still had a chance.

After the first two plays of the series, though, we'd gone nowhere. Both were incompletions, so at least the clock hadn't moved much: a batted-down pass at the line of scrimmage, followed by a pass to Braxton—caught, but out of bounds.

Then we converted the third and long. Out to our 41. We reeled off consecutive first downs on two gashing run plays, taking us inside their 35, still with half a minute to go. Faced with third and long again after a couple of incompletions, Braxton caught a short ball from Malik in the right flat and ran it to the sticks. First down. Out-of-bounds, clock stopped, at the Florida State 23.

Eleven seconds left.

Which, for a kicker like Badgley, amounted to a forty-yard chip shot, to tie and force overtime.

Or . . .

What about we go for the win?

We did have a time-out to play with, but I didn't want to use it yet. I'd burned one with five minutes left, down in the red zone, when Malik's helmet had flown off after taking a vicious hit. Could have been a targeting penalty maybe, which meant he could've stayed in the game rather than be forced to sit out a play by rule, but the refs didn't see it that way. So I had to make a call. Put in a fresh quarterback, who hadn't played a down in the game? On third and one? On the 6-yard line? Needing a go-ahead score? Or should I use a time-out, and keep our quarterback on the field?

That's the thing about making calls. Sometimes you've got to decide. Right now. You don't have a week or ten days to mull it over. But whether you've got all the time in the world to sit and pray about it, or whether you've got about forty seconds, like I did, you've got to be the one to do it. To make the call. Somewhere inside you, inside that whole complicated combination of memories and experiences, of lessons taught and logical hunches, you've got to bring it all to bear on whatever decision is staring you dead in the face. You've got to squeeze it all down and sort it all out—decide what stays, decide what goes—decide what matters, decide what doesn't—decide who you're going to listen to, and decide whose voice is misleading you—decide what's right and decide what's wrong. Or at least decide what's best. Decide what this moment is calling for.

> **That's the thing about making calls. Sometimes you've got to decide.**

Decide what you can live with. Decide what you can't live without.

That's what I was needing to decide that day.

In my headset, coaches were giving me their opinions, feeding me up-top observations about what they could see and had seen from the coaches' booth—information and advice that might inform the pros and cons of the various alternatives in front of me. That's what I wanted. That's what I'd asked them for. "We can either set up this field goal with a run and a time-out, or we can try to take one more shot. What do y'all think?"

The suggestions came back. This, that, the other. Why it might work. Why it might not.

Then somebody—whether it was my son Jon (our quarterbacks coach), or Ron Dugans (our wide receivers coach), or Stacy Searels (our O-line coach), or Todd Hartley (our tight ends coach), or Thomas Brown (our offensive coordinator)— whoever it was, I can't remember—somebody said, "Make the call, Coach."

Yes. That's what the head coach is there for. Especially when he's also the play caller.

Make the call, Coach.

I decided we were going to take one last shot.

Good choice? We'll see. Because a lot of things could go wrong. We only had time for one play. Not a sack. Certainly not a turnover. Malik needed to get the ball and get rid of it. Fast.

Three-step drop, first progression—not to Braxton, who'd been our primary receiver all day (8 catches, 90 yards, 2 touchdowns), but to little-used, and little-expected, Darrell Langham. Three catches on the *year.* None today.

Malik spotted the one-on-one coverage, dropped the ball in on Darrell's outside shoulder, spinning him around to make the catch. And though well defended, he held on and spun another quarter turn, lunging toward the end zone, all in one motion, stretching the ball out in front of him.

Did it break the plane? Before his knee landed? A half-yard short of the goal line?

It was close. Touchdown on the field. Replays in the booth. Five minutes' worth (or more) of whatever they do up there—slowing it down, backing it up. But apparently no single camera had caught it from a definitive angle, at least not enough to overturn it.

We'd done it. We'd *done* it. Touchdown. Confirmed. Ball game.

Our game.

I had made the call—like hundreds, perhaps thousands of calls before, over a thirty-five-year coaching career and over a sixty-year lifetime. That's a whole lot of calls. Some of them bad, but by the grace of God, in some of my most defining moments, a few well-placed good ones.

This book is about my greatest (and not so great) football and life memories and about the decisions I've made along the way. But it's also about a chance for you to make the call yourself. At your own moments of truth.

PART I

PLAYING DAYS

1

Lucky Jim

You may not know this, but I was a quarterback myself. Actually, a pretty good one. At one point in my career, some people considered me the fourth-best quarterback in the nation.

Or maybe it was just my mom who thought that.

We can talk about that later.

But here's where it all started. When I was a kid, my family zigzagged from Omaha, Nebraska, to Broomfield, Colorado (a little town about halfway between Denver and Boulder). In 1973, after my dad had retrained himself from a tool-and-die maker to a computer programmer, IBM offered him the choice between two available positions: one in Poughkeepsie, New York, and the other in Boca Raton, Florida.

I guess not *every* call is hard to make.

That's how I ended up in south Florida as a thirteen-year-old kid who loved playing ball. And though baseball was my favorite, there was just always something about football. Football was where I found my identity.

Like on those days in eighth grade, when all of us who were playing city league ball would wear our jerseys to school on Friday, ahead of the games on Saturday. There was more than one jersey color roaming the halls on those football Fridays. My teammates and I wore the blue and red of the Boca Jets, while the guys from Delray Beach wore the green and gold of the Delray Rocks. Huge crosstown rivalry.

One Friday between classes during football season, while I was swapping out books in my locker, I suddenly got the sense of being surrounded. Three Delray jerseys were pressing in close on my left—the biggest one belonging to Prince Charles Ferguson III, their imposing middle linebacker. With no other provocation than the Boca colors across my back, it looked like we were about to throw down. Meaning, since it was three-on-one, I was about to get beat down. Right there in the school hallway.

Just as I was calculating my next move, I felt and saw a hand gripping my shoulder from behind. I assumed the frontal attack had now been joined by a rear attack, but before I could spin around and try protecting myself, the guy standing behind me said to the guys standing in front of me, "If you're gonna fight him, you've got to come through me."

It was Murville King, one of my new classmates from Delray that I'd gotten to know in homeroom. Murville didn't play football on Saturdays because his family were Seventh-Day Adventists, but he was strong and athletic, and his words carried weight. They at least provided enough intervention to stall the action on that day, long enough for the bell to ring announcing the start of the next class period. I'd literally been saved by the bell and by my new best friend Murville.

But really, *all* of us eventually became good friends. Even me and Prince Charles Ferguson III. Because once we got into high school, we all became teammates. No more competing colors. All we saw were the blue and gold of Boca High.

Football was how we looked at life and at each other. Football was how I defined what mattered to me.

So when Coach Roger Coffey, head football coach at Boca Raton High, told me prior to my junior year that he wanted me at quarterback, and that if I'd focus on only one sport—no more baseball—he could train me to be good enough to earn a scholarship to play football in college, there was no real decision to make. I was football-only from that time forward.

For me, football was simply who I was.

In fact, I remember Coach Coffey asking me one time if I believed in God. I'm not sure why he asked me that. Maybe he sensed my priorities were out of whack. "I don't know, Coach," I said, "but I'll tell you what I *do* believe in. I believe in football."

I thought he'd be proud of that. But the look on his face wasn't the look of approval I expected. He didn't really say anything. In hindsight, maybe he thought he'd created a monster. Maybe he was right.

But I learned so much from Coach Coffey. He taught me how to be a quarterback. He coached me not just on the practice field and in the classroom but in his home, in his life. I spent a lot of time at his house as a high-school kid—eating meals there, watching game film there, just hanging out with his family there. One of his daughters, no joke, still calls me her brother.

Coach Coffey was the type of coach who made young men out of young football players. He had a rule for us: if any trouble ever broke out at school, which was always a possibility, we were to head straight for the cafeteria and meet him there. If you wanted to be on his team, that's where you'd better be. No fighting. No trouble.

I loved him. I'd have done anything for him.

Anything but be willing to play without him.

Unfortunately, though, that's exactly what happened. For reasons that were never explained to us players, Coach Coffey was relieved of his duties during the summer leading up to my senior year. I couldn't believe it. We had such a good team. We were going to be great that season. But not without *him*. Not for somebody else.

His firing infuriated us so much that when we found out about it, twenty or more players on our team all got together for a big, hastily called meeting at my house. The guys from Delray drove over to join the ones of us from Boca Raton. We worked up a petition that day which we took to the *Sun-Sentinel,* our local newspaper, threatening to boycott the season if Coach Coffey wasn't reinstated. One of their writers, Craig Barnes, got it printed in the next day's edition with all our signatures attached to it. We were dead serious. For the first several days of practice, we refused to show up. My senior year. Without football. Without Coach Coffey. It stunk.

Before long, though, he somehow got word out to a few of us ringleaders to come over to his house to talk things over. Really there wasn't any talking to do. He just told us not to worry about *him.* To worry about *us.* "You boys got to play. You boys got to *play.*"

And, boy, did we play. Right up through the state semifinals, playing for new coach Otis Gray, we were the most successful team Boca Raton had ever put on the field. We lost by only three points to Miami Carol City, who went on the next week to lock up the championship, 10–7 against Choctawhatchee, where Mike Rodrigue was quarterback, who later became my college teammate and lifelong friend.

Coach had been right. There *was* a college scholarship in my future.

I just needed to make the call about which one to accept.

=====

One of the coaches who recruited me that year was Coach Bobby Bowden, who'd come to Florida State in 1976 after an impressive, successful run at West Virginia. I thought long and hard about going there, but in the end I decided against it. They already had a quarterback tandem of Wally Woodham and Jimmy Jordan—both incredible players out of Leon High School in Tallahassee—who platooned with each other for three seasons in a row at FSU. Just didn't look like there was a spot for me there. I wanted to go someplace where the competition was less crowded.

I was also recruited out of high school by Coach Saban—something else you probably didn't know about me. His name was actually *Lou* Saban, but he'd been head coach of three NFL teams (most famously the Buffalo Bills of O. J. Simpson's day, including the year the Juice rushed for 2,000 yards). By 1977, one year removed from being in pro ball for the past sixteen seasons, Coach Saban landed at the University of Miami. Just down the road from my home in Boca.

And I was the guy, he said. I was to be his quarterback in 1978, he said.

Miami had basically been a wasteland of football mediocrity throughout the entire 1970s. They'd lost nearly twice as many games as they'd won. And I was the guy to bring them out of the desert, he told me. "You're going to save this program." Sure sounded better than riding the bench somewhere else.

So I made the call. Miami, here I come. To save the day. Until that day when I was hanging out at the football office—star recruit and his new coach—flipping through the pages of the *Miami Herald,* checking out a list of other football commitments whose names had been published in the paper.

Mike Rodrigue, I read. *QB/DB*. "He's coming here?" I said.

"Aw, don't worry about him. See that slash? He's more of a defensive back."

"Oh, okay." Still scanning. "Well, what about *this* guy?" I said, pointing to another name on the list. *Jim Kelly*, it said. *East Brady, Pennsylvania. QB. No slash.*

"Mark," he said, pausing to put a fatherly arm around me, "somebody's got to back you up."

Yeah. Hmh. *Yeah.*

Good thinking, Coach.

I had lofty goals and dreams. My plan going into college was to start as a freshman, make All-American my second year, win the Heisman my third year, and then opt out and go pro. That was the plan. And leading up to it, even as a high school teenager, I really didn't do anything in my life that wasn't tailored toward accomplishing those objectives. If I thought something was going to keep me from getting where I wanted to go, I just didn't do it.

At Boca High, you know, you pretty much fit into one of three peer groups. You were either a nerd, a jock, or a surfer dude. Not really, but in general. And I was a jock. A jock who was going places. A jock they'd all be talking about one day.

That guy who believed in football.

But what I didn't know was, it's a big problem if your identity is all wrapped up in what you do rather than who you are. When your identity is in what you do, and when what you do falls apart, *you* fall apart.

But the God I wasn't sure I believed in—the God who knew exactly what to do with a guy who believed only in football—must have decided the time was right for taking me through a crisis of identity.

He did it by letting me watch Jim Kelly live out my dreams.

"Lucky Jim."

That's what Mike and I called him.

It's a big problem if your identity is all wrapped up in what you do rather than who you are.

He was uncanny. I mean, Jim was a great ballplayer, don't get me wrong. The 5,000 yards of passing he piled up in four years as a starter at Miami became more than 35,000 yards in his NFL career. The man played in *four* Super Bowls. So, it wasn't like we were beat out by a chump. But I can't tell you how many times, that first year, we'd be in a scrimmage, and Jim would launch a ball into coverage, it would deflect off the defensive back's hands, bounce right to his receiver, in stride—off for a touchdown. I'd go in there next series, drop a crisp pass across the middle, the receiver would muff it, and the ball would glance into the hands of a DB, who'd take it all the way to the house.

I'm exaggerating, of course, mostly to rationalize why I got beat out. Truth be told, Jim was tough as nails and threw the best deep ball I've ever seen. We are good friends to this day. Brothers in Christ.

But he was "Lucky Jim" to Mike and me. The guy I would forever be backing up. Because it wasn't like he was going to be leaving his seat unoccupied anytime soon. We were in the same class. Barring injury, I knew I wouldn't be seeing much playing time. Jim did get hurt our senior season, so I got to play in five games. But by then, I'd already lost most of my drive and determination. Lost it? Not really. I'd basically just thrown it away.

Instead of being All-American on the field, I'd become All-American at the nighttime games. All those big-time hopes and dreams of mine were gone. Blown out of the water. The budding superstar, the savior of the program, had been beaten out by my "backup." And yet it was my identity that had taken the biggest beating of all.

But there was this one summer. When I almost found it. My true identity.

The majority of college students, of course, bail out for home in the summer. Not the football team. We always stayed behind to train for the upcoming season. The summer of 1979, I ended up spending a lot of time with a teammate of mine named John Peasley, probably because we'd long been going down the same path. Up until that time, for as long as I'd known him—if I was an

All-American at the nighttime games, he was a Heisman Trophy candidate. We were sure to have a wild summer. Or so I thought. Except John was different that summer. Way different. He'd gone from being this really angry kind of dude, always looking for a party and a fight, to having a real peace about him. It was just readily obvious. You couldn't keep from noticing it. I finally asked him, "What's happened to you, man?"

You can guess. Stop me if you've heard it before—where a guy who's been a rough, tough person gets tired of the trouble he's causing himself and gets cleaned up to walk the straight and narrow. He tried telling me what he'd experienced, how he'd come to know Christ, how he'd become a Christian, even though the change was still new to him and hard to explain. But I heard him out. And though I didn't exactly admit it then, I got it. I got what he was saying. His description of what had happened to him and the peace that had become so evident and so different in his demeanor made a lot of sense to me. I remember thinking, *You know what? That's what I need.* I needed that peace he had.

But I needed to think about it first. And the closer it got to the end of summer, the harder it became to figure out how this desire that I'd been feeling for a new life with God could possibly share space with my *old* life that would soon be rolling back into town for the fall. What would my roommates think—Clem Barbarino, Mark Cooper? What would my girlfriend think? What would *everybody* think? That's what was hanging me up. I was more worried about what people thought than what God thought. Imagine that. Not very smart.

Besides, I still wanted to be a quarterback. Even though my college path hadn't exactly led me to the stage of the Downtown Athletic Club, I still held out hope that I might get drafted after college, get a crack at the NFL. So, becoming a Christian—especially if it meant being called to be a missionary or something—sure wasn't going to square with what I planned to be doing with my Sundays in the fall.

I knew my identity as a football player wasn't what it used to be anymore. But I didn't know if I really wanted to identify with what being a Christian seemed like to me. I thought it meant being perfect. I thought it meant never doing anything wrong, ever again. And as I took inventory of my sins—and trust me, there were a lot of them—I didn't see how I could ever turn things around without turning into a huge hypocrite. I checked down the list of all the ones I could think of. "I guess I could stop *that* sin," I said, "and I might could stop that *other* sin." But looking at some of the other ones, "Lord knows darn well I'm not stopping *that* sin anytime soon."

I guess I just didn't understand grace.

I couldn't seem to make that call. Not right then.

2

Man with a Plan

Coming out of college, I think I would've been voted one of the least likely to ever become a coach. For one thing, as a player, I had a bad habit of griping about everything we were made to do. Complaining somehow made all the conditioning feel bearable. Plus, I was always asking questions, questioning what we were doing. Most of it came from a genuine desire to learn. I really wanted to understand why. But I think it just made me seem like a pain in the neck.

So how did I get into coaching? When it wasn't in my plans at all?

When I look back to how it felt to be a graduating senior, closing the books on what had been a less than stellar collegiate playing career, I had no idea what to do next. My life had always seemed so clear-cut before. Middle school to high school, high school to college, college to . . . to *now* what?

Surely, I thought, it might even yet be the NFL. I mean, I was still a good ballplayer. Yes, I'd had the misfortune of being stuck behind Lucky Jim Kelly for four years, but surely that hadn't turned me overnight into an insurance salesman . . . although I did eventually try my hand at selling life insurance. Unsuccessfully, it turned out, after my boss was arrested for fraud before I could pass my licensing test with the insurance board. Nor did it turn me into a parking attendant, though I did eventually park cars at the Boca Raton Hotel and Club, working on tips. Nor did it leave me without any other options besides bartending, though I did go through bartending school and pass the test, even if not well enough to keep me from being fired from my first bartending gig. I also got fired from a job selling health club memberships when my manager realized I was recommending to customers that they take advantage of the best deal, rather than the one that earned us the most money.

All of those jobs (and failures) would come later. But before I went down any of those paths, I decided to take my longest of long shots at the football career I'd always planned. After throwing passes alongside Jim at Miami's pro day, which left me feeling pretty good again about my chances of getting drafted, I signed with an agent and sat by the phone on draft day, waiting for the call, the one I thought would telegraph where my plan was taking me next.

The NFL draft in 1983 was a far cry from the spectacle it's become today. But one thing that hasn't changed is the abundance of talent that even then was available to choose from. Looking back on just the quarterbacks that were taken that year, we're talking about John Elway out of Stanford, Dan Marino out of Pitt, Tony Eason out of Illinois, Todd Blackledge out of Penn State, Ken O'Brien out of Cal-Davis. Of all the position players selected in the first round—not just QBs but everybody—seven are now in the Hall of Fame.

Their phones rang. My phone didn't. When it finally did, it wasn't from an NFL team. It was from my agent. He said, "I've got good news and bad news."

"Give me the bad news first."

"You didn't get drafted."

"No kidding. What's the good news?"

He said, "You're now a free agent, and two teams are bidding for you."

"Who? And how much?"

The Pittsburgh Steelers, it seems, were offering me six figures. (Six, comma, zero-zero-zero, point, zero-zero.) The Denver Broncos were offering eight, comma, zero-zero-zero, point, zero-zero—a whopping $8,000.00.

I ended up opting for the big bucks. Rocky Mountain high for me.

Having verbally agreed to terms, they flew me out to Colorado to sign the "big" deal over dinner, after which I was scheduled to meet with head coach Dan Reeves the next morning before flying back home. Everything was going perfect, including a long, encouraging conversation that evening at dinner with John Hadl, the Broncos' receivers coach who'd been an All-Pro quarterback with the San Diego Chargers in the 1960s and '70s. I got back to my room feeling good, feeling genuinely hopeful about what tomorrow and my potential future in the NFL might hold.

But it didn't hold past the late local news. The first story of the night—big news flash—was a breaking report that said John Elway, who'd been drafted first overall just a few days earlier by the then-Baltimore Colts, was being traded to the Denver Broncos before he'd taken a single snap.

And you know what I'm thinking? Here comes Lucky John Elway.

I immediately hopped on the phone with my agent, seeing if there was any way I could get out of this deal and maybe talk with the Steelers to see if they'd consider a do-over, to see if their earlier offer still stood. At this point, after being blindsided by the Elway thing, I didn't mind taking a couple of thousand dollars less if it meant at least getting a shot, which sure wasn't happening here behind a number-one draft pick and at least three other rookie quarterbacks, including eighth-rounder Gary Kubiak out of Texas A&M.

"Did you already sign the contract?" my agent asked.

"Yes."

"It's too late then. Just do your best, Mark. Just make the team."

All right. Here goes nothing.

In fact, that was my stat line after taking only a couple of snaps in rookie camp: 0-for-2 passing for 0 yards. But they must've seen *something* in me, I figured, because I was told after that scrimmage to go grab my playbook out of my room, that Coach Reeves wanted to see me in his office. "Yes! Now we're getting somewhere! Gonna talk some ball with the head coach!"

That's how clueless I was. I honestly didn't realize "come to the coach's office and bring your playbook" was code for "you're about to get cut." In my case not just cut, but the *first guy* to be cut, before most of the veteran players had even gotten there. I remember getting off the elevator that day with my bags slung over my shoulder, still choking back fresh tears and snot from being told I wasn't what they were looking for. I was so pitiful that I think Coach Reeves had even shed a tear with me before I was hustled out of his room.

As I was heading out of the building, one of the established roster players who was just then arriving in his pressed slacks and sunglasses said, "Dang, man, you got cut *already*?"

Yeah, thanks for noticing.

The end of my pro football career. Before it even started.

But something happened the next summer, 1984, at the Boca Hotel and Club, where I'd fallen back on that job parking cars after floundering around for a year in south Florida. The Bible says, "The mind of man plans his way, but the LORD directs his steps" (Prov. 16:9). Doesn't mean there's anything wrong with making plans, but we're never limited just to what we think or what we can see. Even when our plans aren't working out so well for whatever reason, they're not the only plans that are still in motion. God still has plans for us, even when our own plans fail. Even when we don't have *any* plan.

The hotel and club would host these giant parties—parties so big that there wasn't enough room in the parking lot to accommodate all the cars. So we'd park them off-site over at the golf course. Then when the guests would come to pick them up, we'd catch a shuttle out to where their car was located before driving it back over.

> **God still has plans for us, even when our own plans fail. Even when we don't have *any* plan.**

But there was another option, which not only proved faster, if you could physically do it, but also put you in line for making more deliveries and (of course) earning more tips. *You could run.* Instead of hitching a ride, you could take the customer's claim ticket, grab their keys off the hook, and tear out at a dead sprint to go collect their car.

Well, after a few weeks of that, I made a surprising discovery: I was in just about the best shape of my life. And it lit a fire underneath my all-but-forsaken dreams of playing in the NFL, making me think I might just give it another try.

I phoned my agent to tell him what I was considering, to see what he thought of my chances at maybe catching on with another team. My chances of doing it with *him,* he said, were zero. He was done. He wasn't interested in representing me anymore—said I had cost him all the time and money he was willing to lose. So I'd now been cut *and* fired. Which didn't leave me much of a plan to fall back on.

But I did have a friend, Larry Cain, a guy who was actually sort of wanting to break into the sports agenting business anyway, and I asked if he could help me. Sure enough, he got me another shot. Best of all, I didn't have to go far to chase it.

See, you just never know what God is doing.

You never know what He is planning.

When Lou Saban had resigned from the University of Miami after my freshman year, they had hired Howard Schnellenberger as our new coach, the man who'd been offensive coordinator under Don Shula with the Miami Dolphins for the past three years, including their legendary (and still unmatched) undefeated run to the Super Bowl championship in 1973. Having been groomed in Coach Schnellenberger's pro-style offense during almost my entire college career, I guess the Dolphins thought I could be a serviceable guy to them. Maybe the frustration of playing behind Lucky Jim for those four long years had ended up having a long-term upside after all.

I'll never forget walking into the Dolphins locker room for the first time. All the lockers were mapped out in numerical order. I started at the lowest numbers, counting up to see which one was mine: #6, #7, #8. There it was—"RICHT"—#9. Not engraved on a custom nameplate, just scrawled in black Sharpie on a swatch of athletic tape. In fact, the writing actually said "RICHT / DEL GRECO," sharing space with kicker Al del Greco, out of Auburn. Still, seeing my name up there at all, it may as well have been spelled "RESPECT." Because that's instantly how I felt. *Respected.* Why else would they have cared enough to give me my old college number? Unless they respected me?

But before those warm, affirming feelings could settle in my heart, Bobby Monica, the Dolphins long-time equipment man, came around the corner. "Hey, are you Rye-ch-t?" he asked.

"Uh, yeah, I mean, no . . . I mean, it's 'Richt.'"

Whatever.

"Every quarterback who wears #9 in camp gets cut," he said, kind of sadistically.

Heh, funny, I thought. He was joking, right? But what I said out loud, a little cocky, was, "We'll see," sort of glaring at him from behind as he walked away, past the next row of lockers—#10, #11, #12—until my eye stopped at #13, where the name underneath read . . .

"MARINO."

And you know what I was thinking? *Lucky Dan Marino.*

It's why I still joke sometimes about being the "fourth-best quarterback" in the 1980s that nobody ever heard of (except for me and my mom) . . . behind Lucky Jim Kelly, Lucky John Elway, and Lucky Dan Marino.

Hall of Famers, every last one of them. Not really a bad lineup to be overshadowed by.

Truth is, I actually did pretty well in camp. About a month into it, I'd taken another of the written tests that everybody in the quarterbacks room was periodically told to fill out, analyzing reads and progressions and coverages and stuff. On the following Saturday, I'd gotten a few reps in a scrimmage against the New Orleans Saints, who were there in Vero Beach doing a joint practice with the Dolphins. Sunday, an off day, passed pretty quietly. I was still on the team.

Then Monday came. As I headed in to get my ankles taped, trainer Jimmy Watson greeted me, not with tape in his hand, but with instructions to go see Dave Shula, the quarterbacks coach (Don Shula's son), in his office. When I got there, he said the same thing my agent had told me at the outset of my NFL experiment: "I've got some good news and some bad news." The good news was, I'd scored really high on that quarterback test. "You really know your stuff," he said, sounding genuinely impressed. The bad news?

"You need to get your playbook and go see my dad."

Of course by now, I knew. Don Shula wasn't any more interested in talking ball with me than Dan Reeves had been in Denver. And he definitely didn't shed a tear with me. This was it. The #9 jersey that I'd worn for the Miami Dolphins those few weeks would be the last jersey I'd ever put on in active service.

My plans for playing pro football had failed. Tried and failed.

But not my steps. God never stops directing our steps. Though "many plans are in a man's heart," as Proverbs 19:21 says, we're not clairvoyant. We don't always know what's best.

No, I never did get to dress for an NFL game with an NFL team, even though it'd been my dream from as far back as Boca High, and it remained my dream every day, out on those practice fields all that summer. But here's what I know now that I didn't know then. The drills that I thought were part of my plan for reaching my NFL dreams were the same drills God was using to plan for my future. The emphasis on footwork and technique that I thought was part of becoming a professional quarterback was actually how God was training me for becoming a quarterbacks coach. All those meetings I attended on pass protections and route concepts and timing and delivery—all to make me a better ballplayer, I thought—were the same meetings God was using to help me become a play caller, a coordinator, and eventually a head coach.

God never stops directing our steps.

In other words, none of that time was wasted, even though none of it took me to the place where I'd been planning to go. Because, again, "the mind of man plans his way, but the LORD directs his steps."

And if I didn't know the truth of that statement yet, I was about to find it out. In a big, big way.

=====

So there I was, at Scarlett O'Hara's restaurant in Delray Beach, the night my boss fired me from tending bar. But I guess he felt sorry for me, because he kept me on for a few more days. Only not behind the counter. My job from then on was just to clean up and wipe down at night. Hard to believe I was the same guy whose job only weeks before had been as a professional athlete at an NFL training camp.

I think it was while scrubbing the brass there late one evening that I found my imagination trailing back, sort of reliving what I'd just been through with the Dolphins. There was something Jimmy Watson, that trainer, had said—I hadn't really paid it much attention at the time—but when he'd stopped me in the training room that day and told me to go see Dave Shula, he'd mentioned rather offhand that I might want to give some thought to coaching, that he'd heard from people around there that I had a good head for the game. *Coaching. Hmm.* You know, even though I hadn't had a lot of up-close contact with Coach Shula during my time in camp (Don Shula, I'm talking about) because of my rank in the pecking order, he'd impressed me. His whole demeanor. He just had this aura about him. Coach Shula was tough, but he was down to earth. Approachable. A man of real integrity, a man of faith, I believed.

And now that I thought of it, the idea of coaching did seem attractive to me. I'd seen the kind of impact a coach could have on people, from as far back as Coach Coffey, to other coaches I'd played under. But it's one thing to see its influence at a high school level; it's another to see it happening at the *highest* level, the way I observed it in the Shula family.

Coaching. It's the first time I'd really pondered it seriously. *Coaching?* Because I did hate thinking I was done with football.

Soon after that, I ran down a copy of an annual publication called the *Blue Book of College Athletics,* a directory that listed addresses and other particulars about all the college athletic programs in the United States. Flipping through, I started making a list of the schools I might be interested in contacting, ones where I might already have some kind of inroad or connection. I then secured a few letters of recommendation from people like Coach Schnellenberger as well as Coach Earl Morrall, another

Miami Dolphins great who'd been my quarterbacks coach during the last few years of college.

Based mainly on the clout of those references, I'm sure, I soon got a call from LSU. Mike Archer was currently on the defensive staff there. He, too, had been a college coach at Miami during my playing days. Bill Arnsparger, even, who was currently LSU's head coach, had been the Dolphins' defensive coordinator when Coach Schnellenberger was there as his offensive counterpart.

Loose threads, but I could see how they were coming together.

Actually, it was a lot more than just that. Bottom line, there was no coincidence involved in my choosing to go to Miami for college, even though it didn't pan out the way I'd hoped. And there'd been no coincidence involved in my trying out for the Miami Dolphins, even though it resulted in disappointment and a seeming dead end. God had been directing my steps. And if I'd have known it, I could've walked through those days more content, more at peace, less demolished when things went south and left me feeling so upside-down.

That's because knowing who's laying out your steps in front of you, and knowing He's doing it for your good and for His glory, helps you deal with setbacks and downturns without being destroyed by them. You understand they're just the necessary, personalized components to His plan, to His process. Despite the challenge and difficulty, He is wisely fitting everything together into His greater purpose for you.

For me, even though I still hadn't given my heart to Christ yet, it did seem my purpose was finally taking shape. I was headed to LSU to be a graduate assistant, slated to work behind Ed Zaunbrecher, their quarterbacks coach. It was a low-level position, but it was a start. It was something. And, hey, it was football. So I packed a U-Haul, finished up my last few pieces of business in Boca, and got ready to pull out the next day for my new life in Louisiana.

Then Coach Bobby Bowden called.

=====

I'm thinking right now, as I'm sitting here writing, of all the blessings I enjoy in my life today. Each of them directly or indirectly hinged around that one call, on that one night, before that one day when I was leaving home for Baton Rouge.

The timing of it was not incidental; it was monumental. It changed everything for me. A true spiritual marker. Because not only did I end up spending all but one of the next fifteen years there with the Florida State football program, working under Coach Bowden, but I met my wife there, Katharyn. Our boys, Jon and David, were born there. We completed the adoption process there that added another son *and* daughter into our family, Zach and Anya. I met dozens of lifelong friends there.

It's just not the kind of thing you could plan, I don't care *how* good a planner you are.

But it's indicative of the kinds of things God can do when He keeps moving us forward each day through things we didn't expect to be experiencing, whether good things or hard things. Somehow He turns them into purposeful things, whether they're exciting or simply mundane. They still serve a purpose. They serve *His* purpose, His purpose for us. And I'm here to tell you, living out His purpose for us is always better than whatever we would've planned for ourselves if we'd have had complete control over all of it. Following in *His* steps, where *He* wants to take us, is what leads us to the people and the places that give our lives their truest sense of meaning and significance.

And, man, am I grateful to serve that kind of God, who loved me before I ever gave Him the time of day. He was already directing my steps as a seventeen-year-old kid, back when I first met Coach Bowden on a recruiting visit to Florida State as a promising quarterback, which is likely the only way he would ever have known about me. And God had now connected me with a key opening on the FSU staff, where Coach Bowden himself was coaching quarterbacks, meaning I'd be able to work directly under him. Chance of a lifetime. Except that by faith I believe there wasn't anything chancy about it.

Knowing me, had that phone not rung when it did—if I hadn't known of it until I'd driven my stuff to Baton Rouge already—I would never have gone back. I would've already felt committed. It would've been too late. And a lot of things would've been a whole lot different in my life from that point forward.

So, how did I get into coaching? I believe God took me there.

Thank You, God!

PART II

THE FLORIDA STATE YEARS

3

=

What If?

Obviously we learn things from our parents. One of the things I learned from both my mom *and* dad was the value of hard work. I'm thankful for that. They also taught me meaningful lessons that were individual to each one of them.

From my mom, for example, I truly saw what unconditional love meant. She had so much love for all five of us kids—my big brother Lou, my younger brother Craig, as well as my kid sisters Mikki and Nikki. She made all of us feel special. I think we each believed we were her favorite (even though truthfully I was her favorite). LOL. And though her love could not have been more complete toward us as her children, she still had enough love to give to every animal that walked the face of the earth. Even today she feeds the deer, the birds, the squirrels. They literally come just to see her.

But as surely as I received an example of unconditional love from my mom, the trait I learned more than any other from my dad was honesty. His nickname at work, as far back as I can remember, was "Honest Lou." It's just who he was. It's how my dad has always lived.

In fact, near the end of my tenure at Georgia, in 2015—Alabama week in Athens—my dad was walking into the athletic complex there on the university campus one day and spotted a hundred-dollar bill, just lying on the floor. Not a five, ten, or twenty—a hundred! Picking it up, he took it to the receptionist, telling her exactly where he found it, figuring somebody would be coming along later retracing their steps to see where they'd lost it. I don't know how remarkable that is—perhaps you'd do the same thing—but I just know I've seen my dad do that kind of thing my whole life. And I know he would never think of doing any differently. In that way I've been the recipient of what Proverbs 20:7 talks about: "A righteous man who walks in his integrity—how blessed are his sons after him."

But though honesty had worked for my dad throughout his life, in doing the kinds of jobs he'd always done, I was about to get into coaching. At a big-time college football program. And one of my biggest fears was what recruiting would actually be like. I hated to think of the ethical compromises I might be expected to make in order to be part of landing top-rated prospects. I mean, I'd heard the war stories. I'd heard about the kind of shenanigans that went on, about paying players and stuff. Was it possible to do this job without cheating? In real life? And if not—if I would be expected to cheat or else expect to be fired—could I do it? Could I go against what my dad had taught me?

Well, let me open the door for you here, just for a second, and let you sit in with me on one of my first official meetings with the Florida State University football staff. I'd gotten there in January and had been through spring practice. But that summer I attended what Coach Bowden called his "Hideaway" meeting—the kickoff meeting for the football year. It was a time for talking with all the coaches about his overall philosophy, about job descriptions, about the specifics of each person's role, which was especially important for anyone who was new to the program, like me. It was basically a comprehensive presentation on how we would go about our business as a coaching staff, as a football team. That's what the Hideaway meeting was for.

So this was 1985, okay? FSU wasn't quite yet at the place of prominence and dominance that they would eventually attain, where for fourteen straight seasons in the late '80s and throughout the entire decade of the 1990s we would post double-digit-winning records and finish in the top five every year. For *fourteen years.*

Top five. Fourteen years. Think of that.

It's fair to say, by 1985, they were well on their way to getting there. They were coming off a relatively disappointing 7-3-2 season, winning only three of their last eight games. But each loss was against a ranked SEC opponent, and they had come back from fourteen points down in the season-ending Citrus Bowl to tie Georgia 17–17 and finish with a respectable record. They were definitely climbing the mountain, becoming a perennial force to be reckoned with.

And here's the culture I walked into as a green, low-paid graduate assistant: Coach Bowden opened the Hideaway meeting with a devotional. Not just a devotional but an explanation of why it was so important that we even *have* a devotional.

He told how Benjamin Franklin had risen to address the Continental Congress in the early 1780s, when they were hammering out the wording of what would become the United States Constitution. Franklin reminded the assembled delegates that when they had gathered together like this in previous years, back when the tensions of the Revolutionary War had been at peak levels, they were constantly in prayer, not sure if their fledgling country was even going to survive. But now that the war had turned in their favor, now that things were looking up, they'd lost the sense of urgency and dependence on God that had once been their first thought every day. It's why even now, because of Ben Franklin's charge to that group of men more than two hundred years ago, that the U.S. Congress still opens their sessions each morning with a prayer for guidance and wisdom from above.

"See, we think we know things," Coach Bowden said. "We're good coaches. We think we know what we're talking about. But we run out of energy. We run out of ideas. We never stop being in need of God's strength and help and wisdom if we're going to be our best at what we do."

With this inspirational lesson as pretext, he went into a discussion about expectations—what he expected of us; what we could expect of him. Number one was *loyalty.* No matter how hot the pressures of the season might grow, no matter how loud the criticism might become from outside, he expected a commitment from every one of us to be loyal—loyal to him; loyal to one another. And he committed himself to the same thing. He promised to be loyal to us.

> **"We never stop being in need of God's strength and help and wisdom if we're going to be our best at what we do."**

Unless.

And here was his *unless*: "If you cheat, I'm not going to be loyal to that. If you cheat, you'll be on your own." Because at Florida State under Coach Bobby Bowden, there was only one way. The right way. And that's what he expected of all the coaches who worked with him.

Sounds like I'd come to the right place.

——

That year, 1985, was significant in my growth as a coach. Like I said, the opportunity itself was beyond anything I could've hoped for. Art Baker, who'd been the quarterbacks coach and offensive coordinator the year before, had left to become head coach at East Carolina. Coach Bowden then promoted Brad Scott from a GA to a full-time position, coaching tight ends. But because schools are only allowed a certain number of full-time coaches, it left a vacancy at quarterbacks. Coach

Bowden, officially at least, was going to add that role to his own responsibility, but he needed somebody there to help him, somebody who could make sure the work was getting done while he was off tending to his other duties as head coach. So actually, the way it worked out, he was there to lead me and walk me through the first couple of practices and meetings, but after that, he pretty much left me in charge. Just incredible trust.

And, man, did I ever value that. And *learn* from that, and seek to emulate it as my career escalated upward. Critics, especially in his later years, would accuse Coach Bowden of being too hands-off, of not staying involved enough in what was going on at all levels of the game planning and so forth. That's not true. He never became any less involved as a coach than he'd been earlier in his career, where he earned his stripes as one of the best play callers the college game had ever known—a riverboat gambler type who deftly mixed sound football technique with a daring streak for the novel and unexpected. Even as he grew older and began to delegate more, he never lost touch with his football team.

But part of being a successful head coach—or a successful leader in *any* arena of life and work—is being able to bring a staff of people together, motivate them to excellence, then entrust those who show the heart and ability for it with greater responsibility to carry out the vision you've laid in front of them. Even if you never call a play, even if you never call a defense, even if all you do is manage a group of men and their various egos and get each of them to do their jobs well, that's impressive on its own. And he was a master at that. I'm not sure I've ever seen anyone do it better.

He made even *me* feel empowered and confident. And I can tell you, nobody was doing more learning on the job than I was.

Another regular part of his coaching routine, in addition to the annual Hideaway, was his weekly "Iffy" meeting. That's where he would get the entire offensive staff together in his hotel room the night before a game and go over situations. Like, "If it's third and long, what are we going to do?" "If it's third and short, what are we going to do?" "If we're on the goal line . . ." "If there's four minutes left . . ." "If it's the last play of the game . . ." Stuff like that.

It was sort of a rapid-fire question-and-answer. He'd toss out a what-if; the coaches would toss back the kinds of plays we'd been working up in practice that week for those precise situations. It was indicative of how thoroughly he approached each game, as well as how he welcomed and empowered input from every member of his staff. It might have looked informal to somebody peering in from the outside, with Coach Bowden sitting there in his T-shirt and boxers, often chewing on a cigar (though never smoking it) or a wad of Levi Garrett tobacco. But it was all business. It was intensive preparation.

I knew my place at those Iffy meetings. I was invited to participate, to give ideas, but I was not there to push them or insist on being heard. If they wanted to use something I suggested, fine, but if not, that was fine too. About my only bit of weight or leverage in those meetings, or at any other time really, came mainly from my being in Coach Schnellenberger's lineage. In fact, I remember Coach Bowden asking me, first day on the job, "Hey, buddy, you got that playbook from Miami?"

I didn't, of course. Those weren't for us to keep. But I did think to say to him, tapping an index finger to my forehead, "I've got it all up here, Coach." That was pretty much my sole value at that stage of my career.

So, by the last weekend of September, I'd sat through enough Iffy meetings to fully understand how they worked. It was week four. We were playing Kansas the next day, #20 in the country. Everybody was feeding Coach their usual if/then analysis. And for the first real time, when we came to the third-and-long discussion, I spoke up about a pass play we'd installed that week, another play that came with a Miami heritage attached to it.

I had noticed in watching film of Kansas during the week that in pass defense they generally gravitated toward either zero coverage (man-to-man) or two-deep zone (also known as Cover 2) where the two safeties play back, and the corners and linebackers cover the five zones underneath. Given these looks, I remembered a play we'd run at Miami that could exploit either coverage and, especially if we caught them playing zero, could potentially be a big gainer.

Here we go now, I'm going to draw it for you.

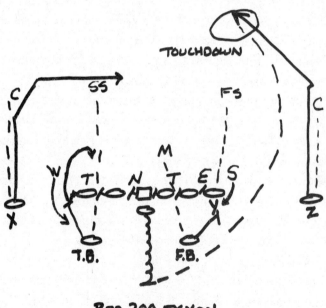

Red 200 Exxon

We called it Red 200 Exxon. "Red 200" meant it was maximum protection: seven guys staying in to block, with a possible eighth (the tailback) if they blitzed the weak-side corner. "Exxon" was just a word that had an X in it, telling the

X receiver (the one who typically lines up on the weak side of the formation) to run a square-in, which told the Z receiver (the flanker, who's generally positioned on the strong side) to run a deep post. It meant we had 'em either way. If they stayed back in two-deep coverage, the square-in across the middle should be open. Even the tailback, assuming they didn't blitz, could release into a short pattern that provided the QB a third option, a check-down. But if the defense came out in zero—especially if they brought the house, coming with an all-out blitz—the Z would be one-on-one with the corner for a bomb, with no help from a safety. Big play.

That was my one contribution to that week's Iffy meeting.

We get into the game, and it's going badly. Kansas jumped out 10-0. We caught up in the second quarter, but still trailed 17-10 at the half. By the fourth quarter they'd stretched their lead to 20-10, and we were scuffling. Just off-kilter. Coach Bowden, hoping for a spark, inserted true freshman quarterback Chip Ferguson into the game. We'd already lost Danny McManus, our main starter, to injury in the previous game, so Coach was looking for anything to get us going.

At one point in that drive—again, with time starting to matter—we found ourselves in a third and long. I'm sitting up in the booth, mainly just to feed information to Coach through his headset about the defensive coverages I was seeing. (He was calling the plays himself at that time, from the sideline of course.) And I heard him pause. It was barely perceptible, maybe just a couple of seconds, but enough time to hint that he was feeling a little indecision. And though I was probably out of line to say it, seeing as how I was sitting up there surrounded by a full staff of veteran coaches, I just blurted out: "Red 200 Exxon!"

Coach Bowden: What? What?

Me: You know, that play we talked about at the Iffy meeting last night. Where we've got the square-in and the post.

Coach Bowden: Uhhhhh... Time-out! Time-out!

He called time-out. I'm now *really* feeling like I've overstepped my bounds. But with the extra minute to work with, I went on to explain the play again, telling him why I thought it made sense here, in this situation, against the coverage they were likely to show.

Coach Bowden: Does Chip know what to do?

Me: Yes, he knows. [I was *pretty* sure he knew.]

Coach Bowden: Okay, then. You get on the phone with him. Make sure he knows exactly what to do.

I did. While the clock was stopped for the time-out, I got on with Chip and told him to key the safeties. If he saw them leveling off, it meant zero coverage, with nobody to give help deep. It meant the post would be there. But if the safety should go deep, then it was Cover 2, meaning he should go from the square-in to the check-down as his progressions. *Got it?*

Now here's where I need to interject something that I didn't know until later. The time-out is what actually ended up doing the magic. Kansas's Mike Gottfried approached me at a coaches' convention the next year and said that when they'd first lined up for that third-down play, they had initially called a Cover 2 defense. But with the added couple of minutes for reflection, as a result of Coach Bowden's time-out, they decided to bring the blitz instead and come full bore after our freshman quarterback. Good news for us; bad news for them.

All I knew at the time, from my seat high above the playing surface, as the defense got into position, was that I could see them creeping up into it. "We've got it," I muttered to myself. "We've *got it!*"

We snapped the ball, and here came the blitz. Everybody blocked, and Chip hit Philip Bryant, a kid out of Bainbridge, Georgia, on a dead run down the center of the field. *Touchdown.* We trailed by only three now, 20–17. After a defensive stop on the next Kansas possession, we scored again, pulling out a 24–20, fourth-quarter squeaker at home to go to 4–0 on the season.

Now maybe, in the big picture, that one single play was nothing huge. Maybe there was another way we could've clawed back into that victory just as easily. But for me, it was truly a defining moment as a coach. It gave me credibility with Coach Bowden and with the rest of the staff. Even the defensive coaches heard this young kid jumping into the middle of everything. I mean, I was really only a few years older at the time than the quarterbacks I was trying to coach. But in that moment, after feeling the excitement of spotting what to do and then watching it develop, watching it work, right there on the big stage, I suddenly felt older than my twenty-five years. I felt like I'd really grown up that day, thanks to a coach humble enough to let a kid sit at the grown-up table like he belonged there, treating even someone like me as if I had a worthwhile role to play.

———

I wasn't the only one. Coach Bowden's legacy is painted rich with people who can trace a lot of their courage and self-confidence back to his willingness to listen to the ideas his young coaches had to offer.

Take Clint Ledbetter, for example. Clint was a first-year graduate assistant at Florida State in 1988. He'd been working with the scout punt team against our first-team defense. And without telling anyone else (as far as I know), he secretly installed a gadget play that he'd brought with him from his days as a defensive lineman at Arkansas State. If you're a Florida State fan, you'll know it by its legendary name—"Puntrooskie"—and you'll remember it being run to spectacular success during a key game against Clemson later that season.

It was basically this. On the snap, the punter leaped high in the air as though the ball had sailed over his head, then he raced back desperately to go recover it—except that the ball had actually been snapped to an up-back, who, while the defense was chasing a loose, phantom ball twenty yards behind the line of scrimmage, had stuck the *real* ball in between the legs of a blocking back in front of him. Are you with me so far? That's when the up-back—the man who'd received the original snap—began carrying the flow of the fake punt toward the right, running what appeared to be a triple option, with another back circling along behind him to take the pitch if he decided to toss it. So while everyone else on defense had starting chasing the play *that* direction, the guy who really had the ball—who'd remained motionless in the backfield with the ball still disguised between his legs—sat tight for a thousand-one, thousand-two count before peeling off to the left, where *nobody* was looking for the ball to go.

Well, our varsity defensive team, when Clint's unit ran the play against them in a scrimmage, bit on it hard. Totally fooled. And Coach Bowden, from that moment, was in love with Clint's play. And was dying for the opportunity to run it. I mean, we'd be in a real game, in a third-and-short situation, and he'd call a play that was almost intentionally designed to pick up only one yard, just so he could get us into fourth down at the right place on the field where he could run that Puntrooskie play. You think I'm joking. I'm not.

Finally, the right conditions presented themselves. We were playing at Clemson, who was ranked #3 at the time. Deion Sanders, our supremely confident, multi-talented weapon, had run back a sixty-seven-yard punt return early in the third quarter for a touchdown—self-predicted, naturally—to tie the game at 14–all. And with only a minute and a half to go, the score remained tied, 21–21. We were facing a fourth and four, way back at around our own 20. And Coach made the call: "Run it."

We all knew what that meant.

I don't think safety LeRoy Butler—the guy with the ball between his legs—ever actually got to the thousand-two count. Or at least he counted it very quickly. But he saw the open field in front of him, and he couldn't wait any longer. When it was all over, he'd scampered seventy-nine yards, taking it down inside the Clemson 5, before finally being caught and tackled. A last-second field goal from the left hash gave us the three-point victory, 24–21.

But, again, the only reason the play was there to run was because of an unknown, unpaid, unheralded coaching assistant who'd been given the freedom to introduce an idea into the special teams playbook that's now gone down in Florida State lore.

"Let no one despise your youth," the apostle Paul said to his young ministry protégé Timothy (1 Tim. 4:12 NKJV). Call them to integrity. Declare to them your loyalty. And give them a voice. Don't be surprised if the whole team becomes better for it.

That's a winning play for any leader.

4

=

One Empty Seat

I n some ways, it was the same as any college campus on any Saturday night, a few weeks into a new fall semester. A heavy throb of music poured from some of the most typical gathering places, which on this night included FSU's old Montgomery Gym building, home to a student-sponsored dance that had run into the wee hours.

It fell on an open date in our 1986 season, between a nationally televised road loss at #8 Nebraska on September 6 and an upcoming home game the next Saturday, the twentieth, against North Carolina. Many of the players had taken the opportunity to make a quick trip home for the weekend, no doubt roaming the Friday night sidelines and bleachers where they once starred in high school before going off to play college ball. Others, like junior offensive lineman Pablo Lopez, who'd suffered a shoulder injury in the Nebraska game, had been required to hang back in Tallahassee for treatment. We needed our big 6'4", 270-pound starting left tackle healed up and at a hundred percent heading into the following week.

Pablo wasn't the only player who'd stayed in town that weekend, however, whether by choice or by compulsion. A few of those players had decided late in the evening to drive over and check out the dance. Around midnight they wheeled a bit haphazardly through the parking lot, where the couple hundred partyers had been forced outside due to someone yanking on a fire alarm in the building.

At some point in that rather reckless pull-through, words were exchanged between people in the car and people on the ground—heated enough that a guy who'd taken offense at something said from inside the open car window dared to make things physical. (Not a good idea against college athletes.)

If only he'd thought better of it. Instead, the young twenty-year-old, who lived in town but wasn't a Florida State student, sped off with a friend, only to come back an hour later, reinforced by a twelve-gauge shotgun that he'd stowed in the trunk of his car.

Sometime within that hour, the building had been okayed for people to go back inside. Pablo had showed up as well, not because of the dustup but just to dance. But when the guy returned and started up the argument again, one of Pablo's teammates rushed inside to tell him what was going on, that some of the players were being threatened by an angry local. Running outside, Pablo hustled over to where the altercation was taking place, confronting the guy who was yelling and gesturing at everybody from behind his car. At that point the young man popped the trunk and produced the rifle.

Suddenly the stakes had grown eminently more dangerous. Exactly what happened next is not completely clear. But the Pablo I knew, though he certainly wasn't one to back down from a fight, was also no troublemaker. Everybody loved him. Just gravitated to him. He was a born and buoyant leader, enormously popular and outgoing. He came from Miami roots and was styled by *Miami Vice*—as huge in personality as in his massive physical presence. If anything, I believe he was there to de-escalate the situation.

But when the weapon came out, so did Pablo's bravado. From best accounts, he sort of scoffed aloud at the absurdity of where this guy had chosen to take such a stupid war of words. "You're not gonna shoot me, bro," he said, hands out, half-laughing. "You don't have the guts to pull that trigger."

At 2:15 a.m., the phone rang at Coach Bowden's house.

The music had just stopped for his Florida State football team.

———

Life is pretty daily most of the time. You wake up, you get dressed, you go out into the world to do your thing. But we share everyday living space with so much pain and hurt, with so much anger and fear and insecurity—with so many possibilities for things to go wrong—it's inevitable that our routines will occasionally be interrupted by something unexpected, by something unwanted. Sometimes by the unthinkable.

Like twenty-one-year-old, NFL prospect Pablo Lopez, DOA at Tallahassee Memorial Hospital, September 14, 1986.

In moments like these, we're forced to deal with realities that hide beneath the seeming importance of whatever makes up our usual schedule of things to do. Questions come to mind that we hadn't even thought to be asking, either to ourselves or to anyone else, not in a long time. We'd been too busy and preoccupied to ask them.

Our whole lives had been tilted toward just reaching the next goal. Pursuing achievement and satisfaction. Making payments on it. Putting money in the bank toward it. Investing sweat and thought and energy into it. Making our little checklists, rushing between meetings, outthinking the competition. It was all taking us somewhere, we thought, taking us toward what we wanted out of life—which we believed was really out there, out where all our hard work and hopefully a few good breaks would one day deliver it to us.

But then something comes along—something completely out of the blue—and suddenly the whole game board looks different. We realize we're not nearly as in control as we thought we were, even as recently as this morning or yesterday. And it rattles us. It unnerves us.

We're not nearly as in control as we thought we were.

It makes us rethink the meaning of just about everything.

———

Coach Bowden called a 2:00 meeting for that Sunday afternoon. The whole team. A lot of the players were just getting back into town from their weekend off, some of them only then learning the grim details of what had happened to Pablo. (This was before cell phones, of course, before emails. Word still traveled fast, but it did take more than a minute.)

As one of the lower men on the totem pole, my job that day was to take roll and then stand guard at the back door, be sure there weren't any media hanging around or slipping in. This was private. A head coach and his team—his players, his coaches.

And our head coach, standing alone there in deep thought, in the well of our team meeting room, was hurting. You could tell it. He'd seen a lot of players through a lot of trouble in his many years of coaching. But never this. Never anything like this.

Up in the front row was the first-team offense, sitting quietly in the same assigned seats they always occupied at any team meeting—with one stark, noticeable exception: Pablo's chair was empty. And Coach Bowden, struggling to hold taut his emotions, pointed wordlessly toward that chair, toward that gap in the heart of his starting unit, before finally coming out with what he'd come there to say. I don't remember it word for word, but it was basically this . . .

Men, Pablo used to sit . . . right there. And none of us, when this weekend started, ever imagined he wouldn't be sitting there in that chair, today. You guys are eighteen, nineteen, twenty, twenty-one, twenty-two years old—you think you're going to live forever, just like Pablo thought. You think it's only old people who die. But look. Pablo's gone. And I'll be honest with you, I don't know where he stood in his faith. I hate that I don't. But let me ask you, if that had been you who had died last night—if it was *your* chair that sat empty today—do you know where you would spend eternity?

That question—as soon as he asked it—hit me like a ton of bricks. I knew where I would be, and it wasn't heaven.

Almost immediately, the seeds that my friend John Peasley had planted in my life that summer on the U of M campus came to fruition. It's like the Holy Spirit was saying to me, "Now is your time."

So when Coach Bowden said, "Men, if you want to talk with me any more about this, my door is always open," I knew what I needed to do: be at his office first thing in the morning. I was getting this thing settled once and for all.

I'll never forget tapping on his open door the next day.

"Come in, buddy," he said. *Buddy*. That was the name he always called you if he couldn't remember your name. "Come in, buddy." I sort of stepped inside and, without sitting down, said, "Coach, yesterday when you were talking to the players about Pablo and about salvation and all that, you said they could come talk to you about it. I just wondered if, uh . . . I just wondered if a young coach could come talk with you about it too."

His tired face brightened. He stood up and came around to my side of the room.

"Of course you can," he said, as he stepped behind me to close the door. Motioning me to sit down, he reached for a Bible that was on the corner of his desk—his *mother's* Bible, I found out later—and began to read some verses to me that I could tell were already marked and underlined, whether by him or by her.

Coach told me how to be saved.

He told me how we were all created by God but we'd fallen into sin, how when Adam disobeyed God at the very beginning of time, sin entered all men. *All* of us. "All have sinned and fall short of the glory of God" (Rom. 3:23). And that's a problem for us, because God wants us to live with Him in heaven. But His standard for heaven is perfection. And none of us can be perfect. So we're looking at death and hell forever and ever, with no way out, unless we can somehow be made right with Him.

But God knew this would happen. And so God made a way. He sent His Son to Earth to live the perfect life we could never live, to die as the perfect sacrifice for the forgiveness of our sins, and be resurrected from the grave.

All *we* have to do, Coach told me, to receive God's free gift of eternal life, is just to believe that Jesus is His Son, our Messiah, and ask Him to be our Lord and Savior. "If you confess with your mouth Jesus as Lord," he read to me from Romans 10:9 that morning, "and believe in your heart that God raised Him from the dead, you will be saved."

That's how easily the answer to that sobering question can change—easy for us, because of what Jesus did. We can go from being sure we're destined for hell, or being not really sure of anything about God or the future or what in the world we can do about it, to being absolutely sure by faith in Him that our sins are totally forgiven, that we're no longer under condemnation. We're at peace with Him. We're at home with Him. If we believe in the name of the Son of God, the Bible says, "you may know that you have eternal life" (1 John 5:13).

So, what do you think, Mark?

I knew exactly what I thought. I prayed to receive Christ with Coach Bowden right there in his office that Monday morning.

That's when everything changed for me. I didn't know a lot yet about what had happened inside of my heart. I didn't understand, for example, even though he tried to explain it, that I would continue to struggle against the sinful habits that were still in my flesh. I wouldn't walk out of there and never do or think or say anything wrong ever again. I would keep needing Jesus. I *still* need Jesus. I'll never *not* need Jesus. But by believing in Him, simply by recognizing and repenting of my sins and *believing* in Him, my spirit and soul became right with God. My heart changed. My desires changed. My way of thinking changed. The things I wanted to be and do . . . they all changed.

Life really did become simple for me from that point, as far as my goals and the focus of my life were concerned. I'm not saying life became *easy*. There's a big difference between simple and easy. But I immediately went from being this selfish guy who only cared about myself, my wants, and my own career to being a man who was Christ-centered, who truly wanted to live a life that pleased Him. I went from being that kid who said he believed in football to being a young man who'd found something a lot more permanent to believe in.

> I went from being that kid who said he believed in football to being a young man who'd found something a lot more permanent to believe in.

It was a tough time for our football team. The toughest. We didn't know if it was something we could get beyond, to be honest with you, at least not in our near future. I'd give anything if it had never happened. But I hope Pablo's family, the people who loved him, as well as all those players and coaches who loved being around him, can hear me say today that Pablo Lopez did not die in vain. The tragic circumstances of his death helped save my life.

It also proves something else: the importance of planting seeds in other people's lives. Because if John Peasley had not been willing to share his faith with me when he did, I'm not sure even the death of Pablo Lopez would've gotten through to me.

I'm grateful God let me live long enough to make the decision He wanted me to make. I'm grateful He gave me time for those seeds to ripen, years after I'd decided I wasn't yet ready to trust Him. I wasn't guaranteed that length of patience. None of us is. I wouldn't be able to make that decision after I was dead. But just as we don't know how long we can wait to get serious about God, we also don't know how timely those little seeds of truth and testimony that we plant in others' lives may turn out to be.

I knew what the message of that one empty chair meant for me.

It meant I needed to make the most important call of all.

5

Hard to Be Humble

The 1987 season for Florida State—the next year after Pablo's death—almost couldn't have gone any better, as far as our performance on the field. We ended up outscoring our opponents 450-135, averaging more than forty points per game. We snapped a six-game losing streak to Florida, 28-14, on their home field in Gainesville to close out the regular season, then capped off everything with the first New Year's Day bowl victory in school history, a 31-28 thriller against Nebraska in Tempe, Arizona.

We easily could've lost that game. The momentum swung back and forth the whole way. We'd erased a two-touchdown deficit to take a 21-14 halftime lead, but Nebraska had pulled back ahead, 28-24, and was driving late to put the game basically out of reach. On a second and goal from the two, our D-line—anchored by noseguard Odell Haggins—not only stuffed the run but popped the ball loose, recovering the fumble at the 3. It left us with seven minutes on the clock, which was good—but now we had the entire length of the field to cover against a 1980s-era Nebraska defense that, except for a ten-point loss to Oklahoma in a battle of #1 versus #2 earlier in the year, had not given up more than seven points in any single game throughout the last seven weeks of their season. They were Tom Osborne tough.

Yet we somehow managed on our final drive to slice through their secondary fairly quickly—a short pass here, a screen pass there, before ripping off a fifty-yard connection from quarterback Danny McManus to Dexter Carter that completely flipped the script. We were now on *their* 2-yard line—the only difference being we weren't ahead and trying to put the game away; we were four points behind and needing a touchdown to survive.

Twice we failed to punch it in, then Dexter was flagged for fifteen yards, kicking back at a tackler who wouldn't let go of his ankle. The personal foul turned a promising situation into a desperate one, ultimately resulting in a fourth and goal—fourth and ball game—from the 15.

Here's where we pulled another page from the Miami playbook: 470 Dip—shorthand for a double-in and a post. The inside receiver ran a ten-yard dig, controlling the safety, while the outside receiver (Ronald Lewis, in this case) ran a seventeen-yard dig route. It was designed to defeat Nebraska's favorite coverage, Cover 4, and it worked.

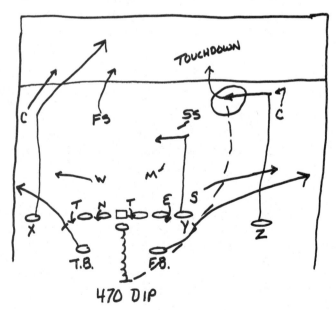

470 DIP

We got into the end zone and sealed the deal. The 31–28 win pushed our number of points scored that season, including the bowl game, to a whopping 481.

If only we'd gotten just two more back in October.

Our only blemish on the record that year had been a week-five loss to (who else?) Miami, a game we led by sixteen in the second half. In the end, though—after *they'd* rallied, then after *we'd* rallied—it all came down to a decision to go for a two-point conversion with under a minute left, trailing 26–25, rather than settle for a tie. Two measly points, in a season where we racked up nearly five hundred of them, was the only thing that prevented FSU's first-ever undefeated record and #1 overall ranking.

But it sure did put high hopes, and high expectations, onto 1988.

====

Along with my newfound faith in Christ came a real desire to learn more about Him and grow in my relationship with Him. Many of the things I was feeling and being taught were all new to my way of thinking, and I wanted to know what He truly expected of me.

I became curious about the Christian practice of fasting. I found it interesting that Jesus, in Matthew 6, doesn't say "*If* you fast," but "*When* you fast." Sounds less like a suggestion and more like a command. Having read up on it, I learned it entailed a lot more than just the physical endurance aspect. There's more to it than just denying yourself food. The only thing not eating does is make you hungry.

Fasting is a drastic cleansing of your spirit. It opens up your heart more completely to God. You learn a lot about Him in the process. You learn a lot about yourself. It clarifies a lot of things you couldn't see before.

I've completed several forty-day fasts in the years since, each for its own specific reason. But the first one I ever did was somewhere during this time period, after I'd been at Florida State for a few years and was seeking direction about what God wanted of me. We were having success, and I was becoming more and more a part of it, little by little, making more contributions to it with each passing season. And that was good. But I wanted to be sure my main goal wasn't getting lost in the pursuit of football glory. My goal now was simply to try living in a way that was pleasing to God every day. If that meant coaching football, I would keep coaching football. But if it meant something else—and I truly meant this—I would do something else. But I needed Him to be the one to tell me. I truly wanted Him to be first in my life.

Or I thought I did.

Fasting brought to mind many sins that I was still allowing to clutter up and complicate my life. Fasting exposed me. It showed me I had a lot in common with that gut of mine, constantly growling to be fed, demanding to be given what it wanted. God showed me in that season of spiritual searching the darkness of my heart, the depths of my pride, the parts of me that didn't want anyone or anything else to be first. Things that needed to be confessed, and then thank Him for forgiving them at the cross.

It ended up being a truly powerful experience. I came away from those forty days, not hearing His voice in my ears, but definitely sensing Him communicating to me, "I created you, I love you, and all I want is for you to love Me back." Simple as that.

But it was definitely a *humbling* experience, as I knew it would be. I'd written in my journal on the very first day, "I see fasting as a sign of a person who is trying to humble himself before God." Humility, the Bible says, is the unexpected path to greatness.

What we somehow fail to realize, because of the persistence of our pride, is that humility is the *only* path to true greatness.

═══

If you were to make a list of individual teams from pro football history who truly took over and dominated an entire NFL season, your list would most likely be a short one. There haven't been many. I'm not talking about dynasties, like the Steelers of the 1970s, or the 49ers of the '80s and early '90s, or even the Patriots of

Humility is the *only* path to true greatness.

more recent years. I just mean where for one isolated season a team was head-and-shoulders above everybody else, where everything clicked and came together, and no other team in the league was really a close second that year.

The undefeated '72 Dolphins would certainly be up there, no question. But you could arguably make the case that the most dominant single season ever put together by any team in the modern NFL era was by the 1985 Chicago Bears. They did lose one game (to the Dolphins, ironically), but they were rarely challenged otherwise. Their two playoff wins, leading up to a 46–10 drubbing of the New England Patriots in Super Bowl XX, were both shutouts. The '85 Bears, man, they killed it.

They had folks like Jim McMahon at quarterback, Walter Payton in the backfield, Willie Gault at receiver, Richard Dent at defensive end, Mike Singletary at linebacker, and, of course, 6'2", 335-pound, William "Refrigerator" Perry. "The Fridge" lined up not only along the defensive front, but occasionally took some handoffs, and scored touchdowns, on one-yard plunges into the end zone.

One more name I want to mention from that team is former University of Georgia and two-time All-American placekicker Kevin Butler. Coincidentally, I coached his son Drew at UGA, the first punter in program history to earn All-American recognition, as well as the recipient of the Ray Guy Award, bestowed annually on the most outstanding collegiate punter in the nation.

Obviously I'm leaving out a lot of other names of great players and coaches from the 1985 Bears, including their head coach Mike Ditka and defensive coordinator Buddy Ryan, architect of the 46 defense.

But if you're of an age to remember the Bears' performance on the field during that season, you also know they're remembered for the vibe of another performance: "The Super Bowl Shuffle," a choreographed rap video, starring forgettable singing and dance moves from a number of their key players in uniform. It is decidedly cringe-worthy to try watching it *now*, given the upgrades in our modern media tastes. But coming as it did from the pioneer days of MTV and the whole music video genre, it really wasn't half bad. It certainly captured the "we bad" confidence of a team that was proving untouchable as they rolled through a historic championship season.

My sole point in taking you on this quick trip through the NFL history books is to put you in the mind-set of the 1988 Florida State Seminoles, who, based on the previous year's 11–1 record, were being touted as the preseason favorite to win it all. The annual publications were coming out, and the hype and accolades were pouring in. This was supposed to be *the* year when Florida State, who'd been knocking on the door the past couple of seasons, was poised to blow through everything and knock the door down.

And to somebody—probably Deion, though I know there were others—it seemed like this whole Preseason #1 thing was worthy of a "Super Bowl Shuffle"-inspired "Seminole Rap."

Let's hope you haven't seen it, "The Seminole Rap" (though I'm sure you've just now looked it up on YouTube). So, what did you think? Same here. Bad idea from start to finish. Deion, who

I love, struck his usual star quality. But our two upperclassman quarterbacks, Chip Ferguson and Peter Tom Willis, looked entirely out of their element. And, bless his heart, poor Odell Haggins—he remains to this day a beloved figure in the Florida State family, but he would probably give anything to have sat that one out. Trust me, he's never quite lived it down.

"The Seminole Rap." Coach Bowden wasn't exactly a fan of it either, as you'd imagine. But he was an open-minded innovator by nature. And by the time he was made aware of the project, knowing the players had already put work into it and were excited about it, he hated to squash it and dampen their morale. He gave the production his reluctant approval.

And, I guess, judging again by the standards of the day, I'll give them an A for effort.

But just know, the concept of "bulletin board material" is not a sports myth. It's a real thing. And you can be sure, down in the dressing room that I knew so well at the University of Miami (our week-one opponent in the upcoming season), Coach Jimmy Johnson was running "The Seminole Rap" on an endless loop.

The Hurricanes were coming off another national championship, an undefeated 12–0 season, but for some reason had dropped to #6 in the preseason rankings—which, again, means nothing, except for how a high ranking tends to make a team believe in their own bragging rights, and a low ranking tends to light a fire under a team to prove their doubters wrong.

I'll go ahead and spoil the ending, if you don't already know it. We went down to the old Orange Bowl stadium for a September 3, Saturday night, Labor Day weekend showdown. And we got our butts kicked, 31–zip.

Ironically enough, in light of the Seminoles' riff on "The Super Bowl Shuffle," Miami came out in a version of the Bears' 46 defense—a new defense they hadn't shown before. We weren't expecting it. And we had no answers for it.

Most of our trouble was simply the element of surprise. They'd installed this defensive scheme during the offseason (which, of course, is the right time to do it), and the majority of our offense just didn't work against it. If we'd have caught them in the third or fourth game of the year, as opposed to right out of the gate, we would obviously have been better prepared for it. But, hey, that's football. They outfoxed us.

Compounding the surprise factor, however, is that going into that season, we had gotten away from audibling at the line of scrimmage. Coach Bowden's experience with calling audibles in previous years was that it set him up for losing a cat-and-mouse game with the other team. The defense would show blitz; he'd audible to something else; they'd check out of their defense; and around and around we go.

When I first came to Florida State, Coach had asked me if I knew of any alternatives to audibling, and I told him what I'd learned from Miami's system (both the U *and* the Dolphins) that incorporated what's called "sight adjustments." That's where the quarterback and receivers alter their routes after the ball's been snapped, adjusting on the fly to the blitzes that our protections could not pick up. Coach liked it so much, and it worked so well, that we had all but stopped audibling as a common practice in favor of sight adjustments. But as it turned out, guess what?— we still needed the advantage of calling an audible in certain circumstances, like against the 46 defense. Because, as you can see, we got the worst of it. Six turnovers, including *five* interceptions. We were never in the game.

Let's just say there wasn't too much airplay after that for "The Seminole Rap." Not in Tallahassee at least.

It was a major come-down for a team that had been pegged as unbeatable and who obviously believed themselves to be. Yet as the Bible says, "God is opposed to the proud but gives grace to the humble" (James 4:6). The path to greatness is not found through thinking ourselves superior to others but by daily just doing our business, keeping a low profile, and quietly believing the truth rather than loudly chanting our own praises.

But here's the thing. This "grace" that God gives to the humble includes the grace of a second chance. He doesn't shame us for becoming enamored with our own write-ups; He loves us enough to catch us on the way down and give us another shot at learning humility on the backside.

One of the main engines behind what became the Florida State offensive juggernaut that propelled us into an unprecedented decade of success was actually born in that devastating loss to Miami, in the shocking embarrassment of an utterly humbling defeat. We realized we needed to continue our ability to adjust routes after the snap, but we also needed the ability to change the entire play at the line of scrimmage. We needed both. We needed an offense that was not just powerful but was equally nimble, that couldn't be outsmarted by schemes that already had us at a disadvantage before we even broke the huddle.

> He loves us enough to catch us on the way down and give us another shot at learning humility on the backside.

Coach Bowden, who was always open to change and to the input of his staff, gave us permission to brainstorm new concepts that would revolutionize the Florida State offense and prevent us from repeating the frustration of that opening night debacle. The change was immediate. We took our lumps from the Miami game, of course, tumbling about as far down in the polls as the voters will let you fall after just one loss—from #1 to #10. But the entire team rebounded, pretty much shredding the rest of our schedule, culminating in another New Year's bowl victory, 13-7 over Auburn, completing our climb back into the top four.

The lessons of humility have their costs. "Pride goes before destruction, and a haughty spirit before a fall" (Prov. 16:18 ESV). But "humble yourselves in the presence of the Lord, and He will exalt you" (James 4:10).

6

Fear or Faith?

I asked God to grow my faith; He sent me to East Carolina.

Don't take me wrong when I say that. East Carolina has a proud football heritage, emerging onto the radar as a Division I independent under Pat Dye in the 1970s. They love their football, and they'd tasted enough success by then to want to see it grow. In their 1983 season, for instance, behind an offense that featured future NFL running back Earnest Byner, the Pirates wound up 8-3, ranked #20 in the country. Each of their losses that year came on the road against the big three Florida schools—Florida State, Florida, and eventual national champion Miami—by a total of only thirteen points.

So despite being relatively unknown as a quality mid-major, they'd built a solid program by 1989 when new head coach Bill Lewis called, offering me the job as offensive coordinator.

He had just gotten hired at East Carolina after three seasons at Wyoming and was shopping for a young coordinator to put on his staff, one who would fit his coaching budget. Having a close relationship with Coach Bowden and being aware of the kind of offense he ran, he called inquiring if anyone on his staff would fit the bill. Coach Bowden mentioned Billy Sexton, his running backs coach, but Billy wasn't interested when approached about it. Billy did mention, though, that *I* might be open to it. So Bill Lewis called Coach Bowden back to get his opinion of *me,* whether he thought I was up to the task of being coordinator. He said yes.

Coach Lewis then contacted another coach he knew— Jimmy Johnson at Miami—not to ask specifically about me, but again just to see if he knew of anyone, someone on his staff maybe, who he thought might make a good candidate. Bill remembers Coach Johnson saying, "That quarterbacks guy up at Florida State, *he'd* be a pretty good one." It was enough of an endorsement to put me at or near the top of the list.

When he offered me the job, it wasn't really a hard call to make. Sure, it was hard walking away from a place that was so established and successful, hard to leave behind the stability and comfort of knowing exactly what was expected of me— the people and processes that I'd become so familiar with. But despite the integral role that Coach Bowden had allowed me to play on his staff, I was still on volunteer status. I wasn't even officially a full-time coach. I'd now be making the leap to *coordinator*, a big step up for a twenty-eight-year-old.

I quickly accepted.

But I must confess to you, the next day after I'd said yes to Bill Lewis, I called him back and said, "Coach, I hate to do this, but I just don't think I'm ready for the job."

You don't need to be an insider in the world of college football coaching to know that what I'd just done was dangerously close to career suicide. When you get a chance as a young man to upgrade your situation to that extent, you don't immediately start looking for the escape hatch. No matter how overwhelming the responsibility feels, you plow on through the butterflies. You stop listening to your self-doubts. You get reacquainted with your confidence *real* fast. You step up into the opportunity that's been provided you. If you don't, word gets around.

I won't go any deeper into how sick my stomach felt or how spooked I'd allowed myself to become at the prospect of being completely in charge of an offense. But to Bill Lewis's credit—and I have a great deal of love and respect for him—he didn't get exasperated with me. If I were him, I probably would've said, "Hey, if you don't believe you can do it, maybe I should go find someone else." But he didn't give me that answer. He didn't wince at my indecision. He said, "No, you can do it, Mark. I believe in you."

Okay.

I'll do it then.

Truth is, as things turned out, it actually did become as big a challenge as I'd played it up to be, only not in the way I'd expected. Throughout the first part of this roller coaster ride, the problem wasn't how to run an offense; the problem was whether or not we could get anybody to come lead the *defense*.

One of the things that had given me a measure of assurance about everything turning out okay was that Dicky Clark, who'd been a position coach at Georgia for fifteen years, had been hired as the new defensive coordinator. He was someone I knew and respected. I was sure we would work well together. But as I was coming into Greenville for the first time, preparing to get settled, I stopped at a pay phone to call Coach Lewis, just to check in. That's when he gave me the news that Dicky wasn't coming. He'd changed his mind and taken a job at Georgia, where he'd played collegiately.

Great. *Now* you tell me. When it's too late to turn around.

Bill then started courting a guy named Tommy Tuberville. Maybe you've heard of him. The main thing I remember about *that* is, my wife, Katharyn, was in town by then, staying with me in a hotel while we looked for a place to live. The night Coach Lewis and I were going to meet with Tommy over dinner, I'd just gotten back in town from a week on the road recruiting. I rushed into our hotel room, grabbed a shower and a quick change of clothes, and was just about to head back out when I noticed a beautiful vase of flowers on the dresser.

"Who are those from?" I asked Katharyn.

"From our realtor," she said, accompanying her answer with a book that she threw sharply in my direction. "At least *somebody* remembered it was my birthday."

I'd say some kind of lesson was learned that night.

The bigger issue, really, was that I'd complained about being lonely up there in Greenville, and I'd talked her into coming to stay with me while we waited out our housing situation. Every week, though, I was out recruiting while she was stuck there in the hotel all alone, with nobody else in town that she knew. It was not my best moment as a husband. She at least deserved a happy birthday.

Anyway, Tommy ended up being hired by Jimmy Johnson at Miami, after which Bill offered the job to Nick Rapone, a guy from up north. But then Pitt offered him a job on *their* staff, and he decided to go closer to home. He then turned to Donnie Thompson, who was currently on staff as a defensive assistant, before Donnie, too, left to take a job with Mack Brown at North Carolina.

So it was a rough go, a rocky start. Finally a guy named Tom McMahon accepted the job and appeared willing to stay. But even with all the staff movement settled down, the dynamic for me remained tense. Because, bear in mind, I'd never even been on a recruiting visit before coming there. Recruiting had been above my pay grade at Florida State. Yet I was tasked now with leading coaches on our offensive staff who were older than me, more experienced than me, and who no doubt wondered at times why *they* hadn't been tapped as coordinator instead of this twenty-something kid they'd never heard of. We're all friends now—guys like Steve Logan and Steve Shankweiler—but they were intimidating to me at the time, whether they intended to be or not.

Fear had overtaken my spirit, to the point where I didn't even want to get out of bed and go to work in the morning. Just a complete feeling of inadequacy and insecurity that was sapping my ability to cope, not to mention my ability to lead.

I honestly don't know what I'd have done . . .

If it hadn't been for Katharyn.

=====

Katharyn.

We met while at Florida State, back when I was a grad assistant and she was still a student (though, despite what Wikipedia says, she was not an FSU cheerleader).

I hadn't gone there to scope out the coeds, I promise you. I don't think Coach Bowden would've appreciated that.

But I had mentioned to Liz Ward, who was dating one of my fellow GAs, Jay Perkins, that I was wanting to meet a nice girl. "Oh!" she said, "I know somebody who'd be perfect for you—my roommate, Kathy."

So we got set up on a blind date. A double-date actually, with Liz and Jay. The ladies were in charge of the food, and we were in charge of the movie. *Animal House*, I hate to admit.

We hit it off and became best friends. I told her all of my darkest secrets, but she liked me anyway. Our friendship grew into a romance, and I asked her to marry me. She said yes.

We married in March 1987. I highly recommend becoming best friends before romance and marriage.

Two years later, there we were. Alone at East Carolina.

And Katharyn's husband was a mess. I just couldn't seem to get the fear out of me. And yet every day, no matter how much of a baby I was being at home, she never tore into me or belittled me. She never accused me of being soft for not being able to just snap out of it. She kept on supporting me, kept on encouraging me. She never gave up on me. "She would always say, 'I believe in you. You can do it.'"

Maybe that's why I could dare to believe that God hadn't given up on me either.

I can say now, that year in the wilderness at East Carolina brought me closer to Christ than I'd ever been. I started praying desperate prayers—which, I've noticed, are not the kind of prayers I typically pray during the easy times, the good times. And yet it seems the more desperate my prayers are, the more effective they are. We should probably pray more desperately *all* the time.

Somewhere I came across a copy of a book that was popular then: *The Power of Positive Thinking* by Norman Vincent Peale. He talked in the book about how we needed to condition our thoughts through prayer and the memorizing of Scripture, how we should let God's Word be the truth that we keep playing through our heads. And in the midst of a time when I just felt overwhelmed by the challenges I was up against at work, I discovered that if I'd keep repeating to myself the promises of God from the Bible, He would back them up by putting His strength into my spirit. He would keep me from failing. He would deliver me from fear.

I don't remember how long my funk lasted into the season. But I do remember the day when, all of a sudden, like a light switch, I realized I was at peace. God and His Word had recalibrated my brain, my decision-making, my emotions. I felt, talked, and acted like a whole new man.

Here's the only way I know to explain it. I don't believe fear and faith can exist together in the same spirit. I believe when my faith grew stronger than my fear, I was at peace.

In other words, we don't need to turn into supermen in order to gain control over our runaway anxiety. We just need to decide we're going to be driven by faith instead. It doesn't mean everything becomes instantly easy. But, like I said before, it does make life more simple.

Instead of fear . . . faith.

Again, I'm not saying it's easy. In fact, I'll confess something else to you, since I've already opened myself up with you this far. Years later I faced a similar battle against fear, after accepting the head coaching job at Georgia.

I was officially announced as Georgia's head coach the day after Christmas 2000. (I'll tell you more about that later.) But for another week, I was still the offensive coordinator at Florida State, preparing for a national championship game against Oklahoma on January 3.

We don't need to turn into supermen in order to gain control over our runaway anxiety. We just need to decide we're going to be driven by faith instead.

The transition involved in winding down your duties at one school while simultaneously ramping up your duties at another is a ridiculously overwhelming task. I had a Florida State-issued phone in one pocket and a University of Georgia-issued phone in the other pocket. And every time it jingled that weird little Nokia ringtone, I never knew what problem or question was about to be brought to my attention next, one that was now mine to solve.

But like Coach Bowden had told me as I was leaving the assistant coaching ranks to become a head coach, "Mark, you can expect about a crisis per week." He was certainly right about that.

Anyway, we finished out the bowl week, losing 13–2 to the Sooners, scoring zero points on offense. Not a good look for the FSU offensive coordinator. Probably not too exciting for the Georgia fan base either. But at least I was down to only one job now, which is really all a man is capable of doing if he expects to do anything well.

Katharyn and the kids (four of them by that time) had needed to stay back and finish breaking down house in Tallahassee in preparation for our permanent move to Athens. It left me alone temporarily in a Georgia hotel, a stay that eventually stretched out to around a month, during which time I was scrambling to set up shop, hire a staff, and begin laying the groundwork for the program I wanted to run.

We weren't having much success right off, in terms of recruiting. A booster had already pulled me aside at a basketball game, telling me I'd better get it going or else his buddy would start buying us some players. I told him, "Tell your buddy he's going to kill the very thing he thinks he loves." As I walked away, I thought, *What in the world have I gotten myself into?*

That night, I recall, alone there in my hotel room, that old familiar fear was just invading my heart. I can still remember getting down on my face, my nose touching the carpet, crying out, "God, I don't think I can do this!"

We'd already hired a staff. Their families were in the process of relocating (again) to a new school, a new city. I was a hundred percent responsible for the leadership of an SEC football team— not just the Xs and Os, but everything that goes along with it. And while I'd had plenty of experience by that time in rising up to meet new challenges as a coach, moving higher and higher up the scale of exposure and difficulty, the full weight of what I'd just bitten off came crashing down on my head that night as though it had been held there, in suspension, just waiting for the perfect time to bury me in doubt and dread.

"I can't do this!" That's right. I couldn't do it by myself. Just as the Lord once said to Moses—"I will certainly be with you" (Exod. 3:12 csb), when Moses was telling Him all the reasons why He'd picked the wrong guy for the job—I thought He was saying the same thing to me: "I will certainly be with you." Once I knew this in my spirit, I was good to go. I'm not saying that coaching SEC football equates to rescuing an entire nation from bondage in a foreign land. (I'm not saying it's any easier than that either. Maybe.) But I'm telling you, faith is a choice we can always make. And when we do, God will be with us. And when God is with us, fear leaves us.

———

God was certainly with us at East Carolina back in 1990. For one thing, we were able to get pregnant with our first son, Jon. The excitement of that news was the highlight of the year for us.

But God wasn't through surprising us. At the end of the season, I got a call from Grant Teaff, the revered head coach at Baylor University, asking if I'd be interested in coming to talk with him about their offensive coordinator position. Not only was the job coming open, he said, but he was preparing to retire soon (he was already serving as athletic director, in addition to coaching the football team), and said he viewed me as someone he could bring in and groom to be his eventual successor. Pretty heady stuff.

But in almost a *déjà vu* moment, the night before I was scheduled to fly out to Waco, my friend Brad Scott, who I'd worked with at Florida State, called to tell me about some recent developments on Coach Bowden's staff. Wayne McDuffie, who'd been offensive line coach and coordinator, had accepted a job with the Atlanta Falcons. Daryl Dickey, who'd filled my old slot as volunteer assistant working with quarterbacks, was leaving to take a full-time position at Kentucky. Brad was set to slide into the offensive coordinator role, and all these moving pieces meant he could hire someone full-time as quarterbacks coach. He was hoping the "someone" could be me.

What he really hoped, he told me, was that I'd come in and be the unofficial passing game coordinator. Brad had been coaching tight ends. He was more of an expert on the offensive line, on the running game, not so much the perimeter stuff.

Naturally I was interested. And Katharyn, who'd been so stoic and supportive of me that whole time at East Carolina, just broke down and cried when I told her we had the possibility of going back to Tallahassee. (She was in the late stages of pregnancy, remember, and hormonal.) Between wanting to please her and being assured that, not just Brad, but also Coach Bowden thought I was the best choice for the job, we packed our bags again. We were going home.

See? There was nothing to be afraid of. God always has everything under perfect control. Wonder why we often find it so hard to believe?

As it turned out, He used my time at East Carolina to grow my faith and prepare me for what was ahead. "Consider it all joy," the Bible says, "when you encounter various trials, knowing that the testing of your faith produces endurance" (James 1:2-3).

7

Change of Pace

t felt good being wanted—by East Carolina, by Baylor, especially by Coach Bowden and Florida State. It felt encouraging. Validating. Being back in Tallahassee, coaching quarterbacks, put me in good position to grow, to develop even more in my career.

We were winning. And along with winning, of course, comes even *more* attention, from *other* schools, who are constantly looking to fill their coaching vacancies, wanting to bring in new assistants with new ideas and a winning mentality.

Leading up to the 1992 season, I got my first offer from an SEC school to come be their offensive coordinator. Having been through the experience of going to East Carolina, I'd learned to be even more careful and deliberate about making such big decisions. Just because the upside sounds exciting doesn't necessarily mean the timing is right or that it's worth what you're giving up in order to go forward. So, while I was flattered, I was mindful of telling myself to be discerning, cautious, questioning.

One of my genuine hesitations, which I expressed to the AD during my interview, was that we had this quarterback at Florida State who was slated to be our new starter the next year, and I believed he was something special. He'd been backing up Casey Weldon and Brad Johnson, who were both graduating. (Yes, Brad was one of my players before he became my brother-in-law, not to mention a long-time NFL and Super Bowl–winning quarterback). Both Casey and Brad were drafted in the same class, a rarity for two quarterbacks coming out of one school.

But there was this kid, I said, that I hated to miss working with, that I'd really been looking forward to coaching as the starter. The AD replied to me, "I can tell you from experience, Mark, there's always going to be the 'next player.' If you want to move up in the coaching ranks, like I think you do, and like I think you can, you've got to be ready to go when you're given the opportunity."

I stayed.

That's how I got to coach Charlie Ward.

=====

A person once asked me to summarize my feelings on some of the most special guys I've ever coached or been around. Deion Sanders, for example. I wrote: "Competitor; supreme confidence; expected and predicted greatness for himself; would not allow his teammates to be lazy." David Pollack, at the University of Georgia, who I'll talk more about later: "Tenacity; didn't care what anybody else thought; was more concerned about winning than making friends; outworked everybody to the point where they got mad at him, then decided to join him; relentless pursuit of perfecting his craft." There were others, of course—*many* others—like David Greene, Aaron Murray, Jon Stinchcomb, D. J. Shockley, Matt Stafford, A. J. Green, Todd Gurley, Thomas Davis. There are just so many great ones, many more than even these. Again, I've got lots more to tell you about guys like that.

But here's what I wrote about Charlie Ward: "Quiet confidence; true student of the game; my greatest leader with the fewest words spoken; the most highly respected player I ever coached; true man of faith."

His story sounds almost impossible. He came to Florida State in 1989 after sitting out a year following high school to get his test scores up. Not many people know or remember that he was actually the starting *punter* on the team his freshman season, before red-shirting in 1990, during which he began playing point guard on the FSU basketball team. He remained a two-sport athlete throughout his college career and eventually, of course, chose the NBA over the NFL, going on to play professionally for ten years with the New York Knicks.

First, though, came 1992, his first season to start at quarterback, and . . . let's just say the first couple of games didn't exactly put him on the Heisman watch-list. If not for players like Marvin Jones and Derrick Brooks and lots of other great performances by our defense, Charlie might not have gotten out of that first game, a home win against an outmatched Duke team that, if they'd been able to take full advantage of Charlie's mistakes, could've put a real scare into us. Give him credit for tossing four touchdowns, but he needed every one of them if he was to overcome throwing four interceptions, including his first of the year on the opening drive.

Little did we know at the time that it was the start of a trend. He threw four more the next week at Clemson. We barely won on a two-minute scoring drive near the end. After another tough Miami loss—"Wide Right II"—he was up to eleven, an interception rate that ballooned to fifteen by the midway point of the season.

Coach Bowden called me into his office after one of those games, in which Charlie had thrown another couple of picks. "Mark," he said, "Charlie's been throwin' a lot of interceptions lately. And I'm wonderin', is that . . . *his* fault? Is it . . . *my* fault? Or . . . is it *your* fault?" (Oh, boy.)

"It's definitely my fault, Coach," I was quick to say.

And we needed to get it taken care of. *Fast.*

I called Charlie in, immediately after that, and gave him the following reality check. He was currently on pace to challenge the team record for interceptions in a season (23), dubiously held by Gary Huff, a quarterback who apparently overcame his propensity for pickoffs well enough to play six years in the NFL. "You are not going to break that record, Charlie, all right?" I said to him. "Because if you get within one throw of it, you're not playing another down this year."

And yet by the Georgia Tech game in Atlanta on October 17, he was still finding the wrong receiver far too often. Tech, who was now being led by first-year head coach Bill Lewis from my East Carolina days, had come into the game on a bit of a winning streak. Their record stood at 4-1, and if they could notch a win over us, it would go a long way toward giving them a legitimate shot at the conference title. (The 1992 season was Florida State's first in the ACC in football.) Charlie's struggles resulted in us trailing by a point at halftime. By the start of the fourth quarter, Tech was kicking off to us after a made field goal, leading 21-7.

Time to do something different.

Like every team, we had a two-minute package that we were always prepared to move into if we needed to go hurry-up at the end of a game. In this particular case, I know, we weren't yet at the end of the game, but it was clear we were already out of time to stage a comeback if we kept on executing our offense at its normal pace. So as an offensive staff, we made the call to move into our two-minute drill *now!*—with fifteen minutes to go.

First and ten at the 20, Charlie dropped back into the shotgun, and he went no-huddle right down the field—6 of 8 passing, plus a twenty-four-yard scramble, capped off by fullback William Floyd plunging into the end zone from a yard out. 21-14. Tech answered with a drive that led to another field goal, starting us over again at the 20, down ten points, with just over five minutes to play. Again, Charlie threw and ran us down the field, bing-bing-bing, scoring on a five-yard scamper. Coach Bowden then chose, even with three minutes remaining, to gamble an onside kick. It worked. We recovered it. By then, Charlie looked unstoppable. Even facing a fourth and five on the Tech 17 under heavy blitz, he found Kez McCorvey in the flat, who deked a defender and powered across the goal line for the winning score.

(Truth in journalism here: The ball actually popped out when Kez was hit diving into the end zone. Had he broken the plane? Had he *not* broken the plane? The ref signaled touchdown, which meant he had. Thankfully, we were still living in a world where instant replay was just for fun, not for review, and where the orange pylons at the goal line didn't have little eyes inside them. Looked like a touchdown from where I was standing. More importantly it looked like one to the ref from where he was standing, and that's all that mattered. We'll take it.)

Maybe *that*, I hoped—that game, that quarter—would cure Charlie of his interception problems.

But leave it to my wife, Katharyn, to notice it might be something more. She said to me after that game, "You know, Charlie sure does play good when he's in the no-huddle. Why don't you just start the whole game in it?" *Hmm. That's not a bad idea.*

Katharyn. Again.

Katharyn, who'd kept saying to me at East Carolina, "You can do it."

Katharyn, who would often ask me, whenever one of my guys was struggling, "Does he know that you believe in him?" *Well, I'm waiting for him to show me something.* "No, Mark, it doesn't work that way. Does he know now, already, that you believe in him?"

Katharyn, who looked on as an interested observer at that Georgia Tech game in 1992 and suggested, "What if you ran that two-minute offense all the time? Charlie looks so much more comfortable in that."

God gave us our wives for a reason, and one of those reasons involves opening our tunnel-visioned minds to see things from a different perspective. We are so conditioned to be proud, so sure that we're right, so naturally resistant to critique, and so stubborn in the direction of our choices, we often tend to resent, or at best minimize, the kinds of perspective our wife gives. We don't see how they, not being in the middle of our world on an all-day, every-day basis, could possibly contribute an insight that we hadn't already seen ourselves.

But as someone who's learned this lesson both the easy way and the hard way, I can say we husbands do ourselves a huge favor when we open from a posture of *listening* to what our wives have to tell us. They don't replace us, but they do complete us. God gave Eve to Adam to be his "helper," the Bible says. And ten thousand years of marriages in the meantime haven't changed His mind on that.

Our wives would be the last ones to say they know everything. (Well, maybe not the *last.*) But they do know a lot. They perceive. They discern. They're wired to receive input from life that often escapes their husband's train of thought, just as we men are wired with strengths that could be of benefit and blessing to *them,* too.

I certainly wasn't the only person responsible for helping that Georgia Tech game become the blueprint for Florida State football in the 1990s, and the truth is: I wasn't even the only person in my own home who was smart enough to recognize it. The smartest thing I really did was just be willing to listen to Katharyn when she said it.

Listen to your wife, man.

She's usually telling it like it is.

People wonder how the no-huddle offense works. It was actually a lot simpler back then, before rule changes came into effect that allow defenses time to adjust personnel to what the offense is doing.

Basically, you have guys on the sideline signaling plays to the quarterback, using code names that you've invented to match up with certain play calls. For example, "44" was a common off-tackle run to the right; "45" was the same play to the left. To indicate 44 then, we might call it "Floyd," since William Floyd, our fullback, wore number 44. When we felt like switching it up, in order to keep the other team's defense in the dark, we might change 44 to be "Tarzan" and 45 to be "Jane," something like that.

So, again, you've got two or three people, usually players, signaling the plays from the sideline. One person is giving the actual play call; the rest are serving as decoys. The quarterback calls out the alignment, which communicates the strong and weak side of the formation. Then he shouts out the play call—"Floyd! Floyd!"—which tells the skill positions their responsibilities on that particular play as well as where to line up. He then identifies the defensive front, calling out whatever code language tells everybody what to be looking for, which determines the blocking schemes and route running.

In our program, everything was typically snapped on one— "down! set! hut!"—unless the quarterback preceded the play call by pairing it with the word "Fire!," which meant to snap the ball on first sound. "Fire! Floyd!—Fire! Floyd!—set-*hut!*" But we could also go slower, maybe to try luring the defense offside or call their bluff, tricking them into showing their hand. We called those "freeze" plays. Instead of "Fire!," "Frosty!"

Everything was reduced to code words, symbols, or numbers that let you accomplish everything you ordinarily would've said in the huddle, except that it provided extra time to quickly change play calls and alignments at the line, if needed, based on whatever the defense was showing you.

Or just to mess with them. Like, we'd come out in a four-receiver set, wait for the play clock to wind down to ten seconds, then run off several players and run in our big group. The defense would be stuck there in a nickel package with their little bitty defensive backs, and we'd run right through them. Or vice versa. We could start out in our big group on what appeared to be a short yardage situation and then spread out all four receivers at the last second. It was crazy, and fun.

It also gave us options with tempo. Just because we were going no-huddle didn't mean we were necessarily moving at breakneck speed every play. We *could* go fast, of course. (We called that tempo "NASCAR.") But we could also run the offense at normal speed. Yet even then, it was faster than the traditional pace of getting in the huddle, breaking the huddle, running to the line of scrimmage. It really opened up what we were able to do.

At mid-season 1992, we were still in the tinkering stages with all this, adding things, learning things, discovering how and when to run it with *one* back, *two* backs, *no* backs . . . whatever we needed to do. Not until we'd spent the next offseason visiting a few places where they were having success with the no-huddle did we roll it out full-scale. Credit where credit is due to Sam Rutigliano, head coach at Liberty University at the time, particularly to his offensive coordinator, Bob Leahy; the late Sam Wyche with the Cincinnati Bengals; as well as Marv Levy and his staff with the Buffalo Bills, where "Lucky Jim" Kelly was quarterback. Each of these men and their coaching staffs were gracious enough to let us come learn from them how to run the no-huddle offense throughout an entire game.

So we weren't the first to experiment with and implement it, though we were certainly an early adopter of the concept. And we definitely took advantage of what we could to wreak havoc on opposing defenses.

It all started, for us, in week nine against Maryland: no-huddle, from the shotgun, from the get-go—our earliest version of what by next season would be dubbed the "Fast-Break Offense"—Charlie Ward running point on the football field the same way he ran point on the basketball court. We'd actually planned to unveil it the week before at Virginia, immediately following the Georgia Tech game, but it was raining hard that day in Charlottesville. We didn't yet know that not even rain could slow it down.

The numbers tell the story.

Maryland: 69–21

Ten offensive drives in the game; ten touchdowns. (One extra point was blocked.) We walked off the field that day with 858 yards—*eight hundred* and fifty-eight yards—of offense: 424 on the ground, 434 through the air. Charlie rushed for 111. Eight receivers logged double-digit receiving yards. Zero punts. Total domination.

Tulane: 70–7

We led by fifty at halftime. And honestly it wasn't that close. Light traffic on the way out of the stadium that afternoon. Lots of people were already at home or in the restaurants by the time the final horn sounded.

Florida: 45–24

The Gators showed up 8-2 but were still ranked in the top ten, already slotted into the SEC championship game against Alabama. At half we led by three touchdowns, then we punched in another on our first possession of the third quarter. Steve Spurrier pulled his starting quarterback Shane Matthews from the game, wanting to keep him healthy to face the Crimson Tide the following week when a lot more would be at stake than merely state pride.

Nebraska: 27–14

Even with a few extra weeks to prepare for our revamped offense in advance of the Orange Bowl that year, and even with their defensive end Trev Alberts terrorizing us off the edge (we could *not* block that guy!), the 'Huskers never really got too close.

We finished at #2 in the country, 11-1, undefeated in conference play, the first of nine straight ACC championships either shared or outright.

Best of all, we went into the offseason feeling as though the sky was the limit in terms of what we could do in the no-huddle offense.

I went to bed New Year's night just being glad I'd listened to my wife.

====

Oh, and by the way, Charlie threw only four more interceptions after we had our little talk—just *two* in the four weeks following the Georgia Tech game. He threw only four, total, the entire next season. Sounds like he was a pretty good listener too.

8
=

Winning the Big One

They called it the "Game of the Century"—a rare regular season matchup between the current #1 and #2 in the country. It was a cold, cloudy, super windy, November 1992 afternoon in South Bend against a Lou Holtz-coached Notre Dame team sporting the same undefeated record as we had, 9–0, and yet they came in as a touchdown underdog.

We lost.

Trailing by two touchdowns in the fourth quarter, Charlie ripped a pass into the end zone on a fourth and goal from the 20, which deflected off a Fighting Irish defender into the waiting hands of Kez McCorvey. After a three-and-out stop, we quickly managed to work ourselves back within striking distance, down to their 14, but with the game clock already reading zeroes, Charlie's pass was knocked away at the goal line.

The end of our perfect season. Dang.

But don't feel sorry for us. Feel sorry instead for our next opponent, who was about to be on the worst end of the best news we'd ever heard.

It's customary, even before home games, to sequester your team at a nearby hotel where you can keep everybody in one place, limit distractions, conduct your meetings, then bus everybody directly to the stadium the next day to get dressed and start their warm-ups. During our ride into town the following Saturday afternoon from nearby Thomasville, Georgia, before a night game against North Carolina State, news broke of what had just happened at Notre Dame Stadium. Boston College had kicked a last-second, forty-one-yard field goal to stun the Irish.

Suddenly we weren't #2 anymore.

Traffic slowed to a crawl along Tennessee Street, the main drag that leads into Tallahassee. People were exiting their cars, spilling out of the bars and restaurants. It had turned into an all-out street party. Our caravan of buses hoping to make kickoff at Doak Campbell found itself stuck dead-still in traffic, right there in the middle of town.

Yet, to say the least, the game was over before we got there. We won, 62–3, our biggest offensive output amid a season where we'd already posted three shutouts of fifty points or more, even beating Miami (finally!) by a relatively lopsided score of 28–10. The only thing standing between us and the gift of new life in the national championship chase was the traditional end-of-year rivalry game against Florida, to be played that season in Gainesville on the Saturday after Thanksgiving. Steve Spurrier, in his four dynamic years as coach of the Gators, had not yet lost a single game in the Swamp.

Just watching it, you'd have thought we were winning in a blowout. Time of possession was in the neighborhood of two-to-one. We held them to minus-33 yards rushing, thanks to six sacks and an all-around suffocating defense. Charlie had another Heisman-esque performance: 38 of 53 for nearly 450 yards. And yet it took him scrambling around to find true-freshman Warrick Dunn on a little third-and-ten dink route (which he then ran seventy yards for a touchdown) to keep us from punting back to them with enough time to potentially come down, score, and win the game. That's how sneaky good and resilient those Florida teams were.

The win against our in-state rival set up an Orange Bowl rematch with Nebraska.

Don't forget, this was still the era of the "mythical" national championship, prior to either the BCS or the College Football Playoff. You weren't #1 until the voters sent in their ballots the next day and said so. Even the top teams, no matter what their ranking or win-loss record, accepted invitations to bowl games just like everybody else, based primarily on conference tie-ins. In this case, however, it did work out to be a true #1 versus #2 battle. Nothing like having two "Games of the Century" in the same season.

Our largest lead was eight—15-7 late in the third—but in the final minutes Nebraska was inside our 5, trailing 15-13, and threatening to score. Fortunately, we held them to a field goal, but even those three points put us behind, 16-15, with just over a minute to play.

Would it be enough?

Bailed out on two different occasions by Nebraska penalties—once by a personal foul (a late hit out-of-bounds), then again by defensive pass interference—we crept well within field goal range. But you don't need to be a huge fan of college football to know that field goal kicking, especially in the closing moments of key games, is a sensitive area in the collective Florida State consciousness. Between the various "Wide Rights" and "Wide Lefts" through the years, there's enough Seminole heartbreak buried in the system to keep anybody in garnet and gold from ever feeling great about putting all their hopes on the toe of a placekicker.

We continued to inch toward the end zone, but in doing so, we failed to manage the clock well. When Scott Bentley connected on the twenty-two-yard field goal (whew!), the clock still read twenty-one seconds.

And if half a minute was enough for Charlie Ward to move the ball down the field, it was enough, too, for Nebraska quarterback Tommy Frazier, especially after a celebration penalty forced us to kick off from our own 20.

He kept the Cornhusker hopes alive to the last play, a completed pass across the middle, putting the ball inside the 30. But the receiver was tackled as the scoreboard clock ticked to double-zeroes. Out came the Gatorade bath. Coach Bowden, with his hair and shirt dripping, headed out across the field for the coaches' handshake, his players cheering all around him.

But the refs were still convening as Tom Osborne, rightly so, calmly petitioned them (ah, yes, like a true Nebraskan), saying that one second was still on the clock when his player was whistled down and time-out called.

The refs agreed. The clock was wrong. Reset it to read 0:01. The teams were ordered back to their respective benches for Nebraska to set up for a forty-five-yard field goal attempt. To win the game.

To win the national championship.

———

I choose not to dwell on what might have happened if that kick had sailed true rather than tailing left, if it had cost us the chance of being #1 in the final polls. I choose not to dwell on what amounted to our doing a poor job of closing out the game when we had it within our power to burn the clock on our own offensive possession.

I choose to dwell instead on something nearly unheard of—the work of a unique group of men, coaches who'd been together on one staff with almost no attrition over the course of a full decade or more. Mickey Andrews (defensive coordinator),

Brad Scott (offensive coordinator), Chuck Amato (assistant head coach/defensive line), Jim Gladden (outside linebackers), Wally Burnham (inside linebackers), Billy Sexton (running backs), John Eason (receivers), Jimmy Heggins (offensive line), Ronnie Cottrell (recruiting coordinator), plus others.

These were the guys—the ones who'd been on the practice fields and in the film rooms, not only throughout that championship run but in the many years leading up to it—who were all assembled together again the following spring, like always, back in the meeting room with Coach Bowden, getting ready for the next season.

We'd been out recruiting. We'd pushed hard through signing day. We'd hardly skipped a beat or slowed down for a second. We were all back in the office now, looking ahead to spring ball and offseason conditioning, including our famous "mat drills." (More about them later.) Coach Bowden, leading the devotional in that first meeting of the spring, looked into the faces of all those men, including me, who'd been with him for so long, through so many battles. "They always said we couldn't win the big one. Now we've done it. And here it is, springtime, a couple of months later, and . . .

"Mickey," he said, "do you feel any different?"

Mickey. What a competitor. "No," he said," not really."

"Chuck? Feel any different?"

"Not really, Coach."

"Billy?"

"No, they just want us to win another championship, is all."

We were getting the picture. Oh, maybe if he'd asked us that same question the day or two after we'd won, we'd have said yes, we did feel different. The night we got back into Tallahassee after our *next* national championship, I can tell you—Coach's first undefeated season in 1999—I said to Katharyn, as we were heading home from the airport, "Honey, let's go the mall." *What for? What do you want?* "Nothing. I just want to walk up and down the mall and have people pat me on the back, enjoy what we've done." Yeah, I felt different *that* night. On top of the world.

But in March? Just working? Trying to rev it all up again?

"No, not really, I said, when Coach called on me to answer. No different.

"Do you know *why* you don't feel any different?" he said. "Because that's not the big one. Winning the national championship—that's not the big one. The 'big one' is praying to receive Christ as your Lord and Savior. *That* is winning the big one."

And *that* is why I loved working for that man.

I don't know what equates to winning the "big one" in your life. Maybe it's reaching a certain level of employment in your company or becoming a leader in your industry. Maybe it's having a bigger, nicer house than most of your friends. Maybe it's your kid being the star athlete or star whatever that all the other parents wish their kid was like. You tell *me.* You know what it is.

But none of that, even if it happens, is capable of doing what you always thought it would do. Eventually, you'll come to that "feel any different?" moment, like we did, and you'll have to say, "No, not really," because all of those big ones are temporal. They end up being like dust in the wind. Coming to a saving knowledge of Jesus Christ is what's eternal. It's forever.

The Bible says, in what I'd say is my "life verse" . . .

> Whatever you do, do your work heartily, as for
> the Lord rather than for men. (Col. 3:23)

I think people tend to get too uptight about what God wants them to do as their life's work. I really believe He is not so concerned about what we do but how we do it and who we do it for. Most of us typically do what we do, not so much to please the Lord, but to please ourselves by pleasing everybody around us.

But that's a setup for dissatisfaction. When we do our best and do it for God, I think He loves that.

Also, when we do our work for God rather than men, it's the highest accountability we can have, because we know God is always watching. Even still, we do it out of love for Him, not obligation.

> Most of us typically do what we do, not so much to please the Lord, but to please ourselves by pleasing everybody around us. But that's a setup for dissatisfaction.

Yeah, we won the national championship that year—the "big one," as the world sees it. That's nice. You and I will often win those kinds of victories when we're doing our very best for God.

It's just that they're not enough, all by themselves.

9

=

Compete!

The challenge that comes with being at the top, of course, is maintaining the drive to be your best, to keep getting better. (Maybe that's why that verse from Colossians rings so true to me.) When I think about my last seven years at Florida State, moving into the offensive coordinator seat in 1994 after Brad Scott left to become head coach at South Carolina, getting better was the name of the game.

And with the people that God had placed around me, it wasn't hard to stay reminded of it.

It all started, naturally, with Coach Bowden. Underneath that genuine, folksy, congenial exterior was a tremendously competitive spirit. He was always striving to bring the absolute best out of his players, his coaches, and himself.

But defensive coordinator Mickey Andrews, like I said . . .

I mean, I already knew how to compete before I went to Florida State. You don't play for a tough-nosed guy like Howard Schnellenberger without learning you'd better bring it every day with an edge. But nobody in my life taught me to compete the way Mickey did. He was the toughest, most competitive man I've ever met.

On most teams, for example, the offensive and defensive coordinators cooperate with each other in practice. Like, when I had my number-one unit out there, it would not be uncommon to ask his number-two unit to come line up against us in the defensive looks we were expecting to see from our opponent in the upcoming game. To be just sort of a scout team. A "look" team. And I'd gladly do the same for him, but—"No way!" he'd say. "I ain't gonna be no blankety-blank scout team for you. I want my twos to win too."

"Coach," I'd say, "we're playing a *game* this week." I just wanted a simulation of what we'd be running against. But he'd shoot back, "*Y'all* can give me a look; *we* ain't giving you a look." Scrimmages were a war. Even drills were a war. He refused to lose at anything. He was going to beat you at *anything*, didn't matter what.

Case in point: I wish you could've been there to see it the year Randy Moss and Peter Warrick were on our practice squad. Yes, *that* Randy Moss, and *that* Peter Warrick. On the scout team.

Randy had initially signed with Notre Dame out of high school, but before ever enrolling in classes, he got into some kind of altercation back home, serious enough that they decided to revoke his scholarship. Coach Holtz, though, knew what Randy could do. And while he wanted to help him, he also wasn't willing to let him transfer to a school that Notre Dame was scheduled to play. So he reached out to Coach Bowden, knowing he'd be a good influence on him. After a little internal negotiating, the FSU administration agreed to let him come, but only if he redshirted for his first year to prove that he could behave. That's how Randy Moss showed up on the Florida State roster in 1995.

As for Peter Warrick, it was his freshman year as well. But he suffered a bad hamstring pull during camp and said he wanted to redshirt too. "No way," I told him. It was too early to make a call like that. He was too good a player to be riding the bench. I said, "When you're healthy by week three, you're gonna be out there helping us win games. You're too much of a baller, man. We need you.

"Plus," I said, "you know you'll never stay here all four years, much less five, if we let you sit one out now."

"Yes, I will, Coach." *Fat chance*, I thought. But we agreed to redshirt him anyway, as he requested. And that's how we spent an entire fall with the greatest scout-team receivers who ever lived. Two first-round draft picks. On our *scout* team.

I can still see Mickey Andrews cussing and snake-spitting right now. Man, he *hated* watching them torch his defense in practice. He was so mad about it that he asked Coach Bowden if he could take one of our running backs and move him to corner, just to give him at least a puncher's chance at running track with these guys during scrimmages. Nobody could cover them. They were incredible. And it just about drove Mickey out of his mind.

Competitive? Always wanting to be better? Never to lose? Even to ourselves?

It was just baked into the culture.

Even on a personal level, man to man. Do you remember the old *Superstars* competition that used to run on weekend television in the wintertime, after the pro football season ended? Athletes from different sports—football, baseball, basketball, even Olympic sports—would challenge each other in various events, including a final obstacle course that featured rope climbing over a wall, a running long-jump, a couple of hurdles, things like that.

We decided to do something similar when I was at Florida State. I always tried to have a fun, informal get-together with the QBs each spring, and one year we attempted our own version of *Superstars*. Our events were a little different than the ones on TV. We did horseshoes, darts, two-man volleyball, one-on-one basketball, eight-ball, bowling, closest-to-the-pin golf driving, and of course a few football skill events, too, like throwing short-range passes through a tire or throwing a long pass into a garbage can. (The distance on the long ball was determined by how far

I could throw it myself. All I wanted was an unfair advantage. Plus, I was the coach, so I could set the rules.) We developed a scoring system for each event, and the guy who pulled down the highest total score, over all events, was declared the winner.

Well, the contest really caught on. "The Quarterback Classic," as it came to be known, became an annual event, complete not just with bragging rights but with its own plaque or trophy inscribed with the winner's name each year. It even morphed from a contest between current players to a highly anticipated reunion of former players, further stoking the competitive fire. Brad Johnson got so into it that he began writing these snarky, poorly rhyming poems that he sent out before each year's competition, saying things like . . .

> Accuracy, determination, and handling the pressure is what it takes.

> I just want you to know I'm off the Mountain Dew and even the Debbie Cakes.

> So, be at your best and ready to shine.

> Fellows, I will be the champion of the QBs, no doubt in my mind.

(Please.)

Truth be told, Brad did probably win about half of them. Casey Weldon, Peter Tom Willis, and maybe Danny McManus won a time or two as well. (Danny's victory was accompanied by a formal protest from Casey, if I recall.) Heck, I even won a couple myself, believe it or not. But many others participated— Chip Ferguson, Kenny Felder, Danny Kanell, Thad Busby, Marcus Outzen, Chris Weinke, Charlie Ward. One year included an epic showdown between Charlie (NBA star) and Brad (all

6'6" of him)—each of whom had been starters on the Florida State basketball team—going down to the wire on a dirt court with a makeshift goal at my in-laws' house on the outskirts of Tallahassee. Charlie won the battle, but Brad won the war: the overall trophy.

Even after I went to Georgia, the guys insisted on moving the show to Athens, where we incorporated Bulldog QBs into the crossfire as well. It was an exclusive event, only the Coach Richt quarterback family. Part of that family included the quarterback equipment managers, kids who never got the credit they deserved, even though I used to like to tell them they had the easiest job in America. They only had to carry around a bag of balls; all the other equipment guys had to carry the heavy stuff. Guys like "Junior," "Pappy," "Goo III," "Baby Face," his younger brother "Face," and "Billy the Kid." Having a great nickname is a badge of honor, for sure!

Of course the best part of the "Classic" was the male bonding that went on. We call it "Men's Town" in our family. If we're going off with just the guys, we say we're going to "Men's Town." But men need this kind of brotherhood, especially in terms of growing in our faith. We tend to want to do things on our own. We hate to admit our shortcomings and fears. But as men, as friends, if we'll get past the fear of what being together might reveal about us—about the real things going on inside us—this is where we become better, become stronger. "Iron sharpens iron," as the Bible says. "One man sharpens another" (Prov. 27:17). The desire to keep challenging ourselves, to call out the best in each other, isn't a process that ends when our playing days are over. We keep on. We keep working. We stay in shape for the fight. Together. That's how we do it.

The embodiment of our undying commitment to competition at Florida State was the classic 1994 game against Florida, the incomparable "Choke at Doak." Personally, the date was memorable enough to me already, Katharyn was nine-months pregnant and due with our son David on that very Saturday. But then the game itself. *Wow.*

We were behind 31–3 in the fourth quarter, completely shut down. Some of the Gator starters had literally come out of their shoulder pads to watch the second-teamers finish the game. That's how bad it was. It was my first year as coordinator; I was making a good case for it being my last.

Danny Kanell had taken over for Charlie Ward at quarterback—great player, but more of a traditional pocket passer than Charlie had been. We'd gone back to being more I-formation, run-oriented, play-action pass, stuff like that. But none of it was working that day. And in the locker room at halftime, I swear it looked like Coach Bowden was already over there writing notes to himself for how he was going to explain losing to Florida by fifty at home.

"Coach," I said, "we've got to go fast-pace the rest of the game."

"Do what you gotta do," he told me.

And so, we did it again, just like at Georgia Tech in '92. We scrapped the methodical, pounding, power-game offense and, even with Danny in there, we cranked it wide open. Two-minute, up-tempo, no-huddle. No choice.

We started to get things rolling in the third quarter but couldn't seem to generate any points out of it. At the start of the fourth, we were driving. We scored, we scored, we scored. Stopped them, then scored again. And it's not like we were getting lucky breaks and turnovers. It's just that as we got closer, Spurrier couldn't afford to stay conservative and chew up clock.

Suddenly, in a game they'd been leading by four touchdowns, they were fighting to be sure they didn't lose.

After tying it, we even got the ball *back* and were driving again when Danny got caught scrambling, was tackled in bounds short of the first down, and we weren't able to get our field goal unit out onto the field in time. The result was a tie (the college game hadn't adopted overtime rules yet), but it felt like the greatest victory we'd ever pulled off, as if we'd come back from the dead. Then, in a fancy bit of college football marketing, our same two teams were pitted together a month later in the Sugar Bowl in New Orleans for a rematch, billed as "The Fifth Quarter in the French Quarter," which we won close.

It was part of always being better.

Every year, we were all about getting better.

No matter where you are, strive to be your best.

━━━━

One more quick thing on Mickey Andrews and the culture Coach Bowden cultivated at Florida State. Mickey was notorious for getting onto his players. I don't care if you were a Thorpe Award winner like Deion Sanders or Terrell Buckley, he would lay into you like nobody's business.

But *off* the field . . . father, grandfather, whatever you want to call it. When my kids would come for family nights (sort of a picnic supper we had every Sunday night in season for all the coaches and families to get together), they'd make a bee-line for Coach Mickey's office, knowing there'd be some candy waiting for them. As withering as he could be to his players during practice, that's how gentle of a man you'd find him anywhere else. Once you got to understand him, you couldn't help loving him.

But, really, that's the way it worked with *all* the coaches. I don't think it would surprise you to learn, among competitive men, we could sometimes get cross-ways. Work with a guy long enough, and there'll be moments when you irritate the daylights out of one another. You get to know each other's warts.

But you also know each other's hearts—especially when every man, at every morning's staff meeting, is required to take a turn leading a devotional for his fellow coaches. Not everybody was a Christian. You could talk about anything you wanted, as long as it was generally inspirational. But I'd sit there on some days, listening to a guy I'd maybe been angry with, hearing something come out of his mouth, out of his heart, that made me think, okay, "Maybe I don't hate his guts like I did yesterday."

Those staff devotionals that Coach Bowden had us share with one another each morning were the greatest team-building tool of all.

Whenever I talk on leadership, I tell people those staff devotionals that Coach Bowden had us share with one another each morning were the greatest team-building tool of all. It's how we got to trust each other, forgive each other, really *know* each other. We could still argue our points—and we did! But in the end, we were family. We really were. Tough, competitive, but tight-knit.

A real team.

━━━

A coach never calls a perfect game. You never display flawless strategy. You always rethink and critique yourself. But I made some calls that I really wish I could take back in the 1998 national championship game, the first BCS matchup in NCAA history.

One of them happened early, near the start of the second quarter, but it proved to be a turning point in the game. Though we clawed back and made it close, we never overcame that critical play.

A little context: Chris Weinke, our sophomore quarterback who'd retained his eligibility after playing six years of professional baseball, had suffered a serious neck injury late in the season. It hadn't seemed all that bad in the moment, but we later learned he'd come within inches of maybe being in a wheelchair for the rest of his life. It eventually required spinal surgery, fusing two vertebrae in his neck and removing a bone chip that had gotten lodged among the delicate nerves in his spine. The fact that he ever put on a uniform again was a miracle. The fact that he won a Heisman Trophy in it—proof of what comes from fighting to be your best.

So with Wink out, we turned to his backup, Marcus Outzen— "Rooster"—a gutsy, red-haired, 6'2", 220-pound guy who played his tail off to get us through the next two games and into that inaugural BCS championship against Tennessee.

Fiesta Bowl. Tempe, Arizona. January 4, 1999.

Trailing 7-0 and driving at midfield, I called a play that had Peter Warrick going in motion to the right. It was really our only set where we used motion like that. In fact, I don't think we'd ever actually run that play in a game. We'd *practiced* it. But in motion, you expect the corners to back off a little bit, giving the receiver some space underneath. They can't press a moving target. The idea was for Peter to push up the field, keep the corner backpedaling, and then cut off his route, run a simple speed-out to the sideline. It takes a good pass, well-timed, leading the receiver, but it's a sound concept. On its own, it wasn't a bad play call.

But like I told you—and again, this was not very smart of me—the only play we ran in practice from that motion set was Peter doing the little speed-out. Maybe if I'd thought to have him alter his route into an out-and-up, try getting the corner to bite, and then blow right past him, things would've worked out differently. Instead we ran it as ordered, exactly as called, just the way we'd practiced it. I thought it would work.

Anyway, the pass arrived a little behind Pete, but I don't know if it really would've mattered. Dwayne Goodrich, the Tennessee corner, had already sold out on it. He picked it clean, and ran fifty-five yards untouched for the score, putting the Vols up 14-0, a lead they never relinquished.

My bigger mistake—bigger than the result of that single play—was that I just didn't involve Peter enough in what we did on offense that night. He was so dynamic, just a freak of athletic ability. And yet I think he only got one or two balls thrown to him: one catch for seven yards. And the one we shouldn't have thrown to him probably cost us the ball game. Wasn't my best night's work, not in *my* mind. Probably not in a lot of people's minds.

That's the way Peter's junior year ended, his fourth year in the program. And like I told you, I didn't see any way he was coming back and not turning pro, most likely as a first-round draft pick. It shocked not just me but the entire football world when he declared his intention to stay and play out his last year of eligibility. But he'd told me he would, remember? Even when I hadn't believed him. Sure enough, he wanted another shot at winning a championship.

And, boy, I did too.

> Getting better, being your best, is often simply finding the courage (and humility) to learn from your mistakes.

Getting better, being your best, is often simply finding the courage (and humility) to learn from your mistakes. And Pete and I—we were both about to get a big lesson in that.

=====

Peter's decision to delay his shot at earning NFL money was paying off big-time for our 1999 team. We were rolling at 5-0 and holding our lock on the preseason #1 ranking. Pete was leading the mid-season discussion for Heisman Trophy honors, racking up 500 receiving yards and four touchdowns, to go along with two rushing touchdowns, a punt return for a touchdown, even a *passing* touchdown. He was lighting it up.

Then it all went to pieces. He and a teammate, Laveranues Coles, were charged with grand theft after paying around twenty dollars for more than four hundred dollars' worth of designer-label clothes at a Tallahassee department store. The sales clerk, only nineteen, a young girl, admitted to voiding out the real prices and practically giving them the merchandise. She knew they were star athletes. She'd seen them at parties around campus. Turned out, this little price-shaving thing had happened a couple of other times before, between the three of them.

It was clearly wrong. Peter had made a big mistake. And he knew it. After being just the model of hard work and leadership throughout the entire spring and summer and into the regular season, he'd now made a costly lapse in judgment, and was about to pay dearly for it.

That's because in technical terms, the cash he'd paid below their asking price exceeded the $300 maximum for petty theft. It fell into the range of being a felony. And by school policy, any student arrested for a felony, even if the charges were still pending, was immediately suspended from all team activities.

Peter was out.

He sat the Miami game (a win, thank goodness). He sat the Wake Forest game, another win to keep us undefeated. Next up was a road game against Clemson—the first of nine "Bowden Bowls" between Coach and his son Tommy, who was then in his first year at the helm of the Tigers. All the while, negotiations were racing through the halls and phone lines and meeting rooms of local government, as well as the Florida State campus, seeing if any bargain could be reached that would reduce the charges against Pete to a misdemeanor, thus clearing him to play.

What a day. We were literally sitting at the airport, holding the plane, waiting to hear what the people in authority had decided. Finally, the call came in. From the sound of it, it looked like Peter would be picking up trash on the shoulder of the highway for a long time after the season was over. But he would be playing in a Florida State uniform on that Saturday in Clemson.

Still, we only eked it out, 17–14. We'd been behind 14–3 at the half, had rallied back to take the lead with five minutes to play, then Clemson's kicker came up short on a forty-two-yard field goal that would've tied the game and likely sent it into overtime. But we survived and advanced, on a day when #3 Nebraska lost, #9 Michigan lost, #10 Alabama lost, and #11 Michigan State lost. Upset fever was apparently in the air that day, but we managed to escape without poisoning our perfect record.

We then got past Virginia, past Maryland, past Florida by seven, with Peter again putting up the kind of numbers that made him such a torment to opposing defenses.

We'd taken the scenic route, but we'd made it back—back to the BCS championship, to be held that year at the Sugar Bowl in New Orleans, against #2 and undefeated Virginia Tech.

I knew we were in trouble that night when I was out on the field during pregame, before going up to my customary seat in the booth. I'd been around enough elite athletes by that time to grow accustomed to what raw skill looked like. I was hard to impress. Immune to amazement. But at my first real-live sighting of Michael Vick, I was instantly taken aback.

Just *looking* at him, at his physique, all ripped and intense, I wondered how in the world we could slow down a force of nature like that.

Well, you don't beat Michael Vick by keeping the ball out of the hands of Peter Warrick, I'll tell you that. I'd at least learned *that* much in the calendar year, since allowing his stat line to be contained to single digits in a championship game.

Weinke connected with Pete on a first-quarter bomb, sixty-four yards for a touchdown. Early in the second, he ran a punt back sixty yards for another. After our twenty-one-point lead evaporated in the third quarter and Ron Dugans caught a fourteen-yard pass for the go-ahead score, Peter then caught the two-point conversion that put us back up by seven.

Finally, with about eight minutes left, we dialed him up again. Wink sailed one from beyond the 40, connecting with Peter right at the goal line. With a defender's hands wedged between Pete's hands and the ball—flagrant enough to draw a pass interference flag—he gripped it, lost it, popped it up in the air, then secured it as he landed laid-out in the end zone. Human highlight reel.

He had come back for another season to win that ring. His path had turned all sideways in the middle. But given the chance to step back out onto the road again, he had never let up until he'd gotten what he came for.

Always getting better. Always doing more. Never settling. Never stopping. Just getting back up and getting back in the game.

Those are the kind of calls you have to make. On a regular, all-the-time basis. Is today going to be better than yesterday? Will I let past regrets weigh me down so much that I no longer see a future for myself? Have I decided God's gotten tired of me, tired of how I've been living, tired enough that He's finished putting any effort into helping me anymore?

Life is about learning, changing, adjusting, developing. Continuing to put yourself out there and try again. These are the kinds of truths that got burned into my mind over fifteen seasons with Coach Bowden and Florida State. Lessons about diligence, and determination, and family, and commitment, and listening, and humility, and authenticity—about knowing the difference between the "big one" and the *truly* Big One.

I would need all of those qualities and more for the new level of challenges and responsibility awaiting me.

Life is about learning, changing, adjusting, developing. Continuing to put yourself out there and try again.

PART III

THE GEORGIA YEARS

10

Finish the Drill

After the 1996 season, I was interviewed by Pitt for their head coaching vacancy, following Johnny Majors's resignation from his second stint there. They brought us in, showed us around, pointed out the house they provided on campus for the head coach to live in. But Katharyn and I had promised each other we wouldn't make any decision—yes or no—until we got back home to talk and pray about it. I knew we would get treated like a recruit and would need a cool-down period.

As we headed out of Pittsburgh, just the two of us, she was feeling pretty positive about it. I said, "Well, just know, if we say yes, we're saying we want to live here for the rest of our lives." I'd seen what it looks and feels like to remain at one place, the way Coach Bowden had done at Florida State. That's what I wanted for myself as well. I never wanted to go into a team meeting, after accepting a job at another school, and tell my players, "Fellas, I love you, and I appreciate you helping me get where I really want to be . . . which is not here with you." I just wasn't going to do that.

I mean, forgive me for overthinking it maybe, but a lot of the guys who play college football have already seen the men in their lives leave them. Someone they counted on, one of their male role models, walked out on them. And I didn't want to be another one. I wanted players to be able to come back home to their alma mater, years down the road, and know there'd be a familiar face there to greet them.

So when I was beginning to entertain head coaching offers, I was determined not to take a job where I knew eventually I'd be looking for another one. Whenever I went somewhere, I intended to go there to stay.

"*Where* then?" Katharyn asked me. "What's a place where you could see yourself staying for a long time like that?"

Well, I said, thinking through some of the schools that had been open in recent years, the ones that had crossed my mind as desirable destinations, "like a Clemson, or like . . .

"Like Georgia."

━━

Choosing to remain at Florida State had proven a solid decision. I wasn't in a hurry to leave anyway. I loved our players and I loved Coach Bowden. In order for me to think about leaving to become a head coach, it would need to be a special place, somewhere that was awesome for my family and somewhere that I believed the team could win big. By remaining at Florida State, I'd been able to coach another Heisman Trophy candidate, to experience another national championship. Waiting, being patient, being slow to jump at things, is quite often the straightest shot to finding yourself exactly where you want to be. Many times you're already there; you just don't know it.

Being slow to jump at things is quite often the straightest shot to finding yourself exactly where you want to be. Many times you're already there; you just don't know it.

But as 2000 began winding down, as the coaching carousel began swinging into action, I selectively started listening. Virginia interviewed me. Butch Davis, too, had just resigned from Miami, taking the head coaching job with the Cleveland Browns, and people were working to set up an interview for me with Paul Dee, Miami's then-athletic director.

In New York that winter, though, while in town for the Heisman presentation, I met Coach Vince Dooley for the first time. He asked if I'd be interested in meeting privately, there at his room in the Waldorf Astoria, to discuss the head coaching vacancy at the University of Georgia. I went up with him. We were just beginning to chat—I don't think it had been even a minute yet—when his phone rang. He listened for a second, then said, "What? How'd you know that?" When he hung up, he was hot.

He immediately confronted me: "That was a reporter asking if you were in the hotel room with me right now talking about this job. Did you tell anybody about this?"

Honestly, I was as confused as *he* was. It seems my agent had purposely leaked the information, thinking it would be good publicity for me if word got out that I was being courted by an SEC school. (Wasn't long before I fired that agent, by the way.) But in the moment, I was petrified. I thought the whole deal was blown on the spot. I was thinking it was over. "Coach, I'm sorry, I have no idea how that happened." I really didn't.

But soon thereafter, he invited me to a follow-up meeting with himself as well as the school president, Michael Adams. It seemed to go well. Near the end, in fact, when they asked the "do you have any questions for *us*?" bit, I said, "Yes, I do. You hear rumors of recruiting being a little dirty in the SEC. Do you think a program can win without that kind of stuff?" *Absolutely,* Coach Dooley assured me. "Good," I said, "because if you give me this job, that's how we're going to do it."

They told me it would be a few days before I heard back from them, that they had a couple of other people to interview. Fine. I guess that's why I wasn't quite prepared when Coach Dooley called the very next day and made me an offer. It just caught me off-guard. I thanked him. I told him I appreciated it, but, "Coach, I don't know," I said. "I need to think about it just a little."

"Uh . . . all right," he said. "Well . . . what if I offered you another . . ."

"No, Coach, no, I'm not trying to negotiate, I promise you. I just really need a little time to be sure it's the right thing for me to do."

This obviously wasn't the response he was anticipating or accustomed to getting. And he was probably right not to expect it. My brother Craig, when I talked with him soon thereafter, said, "What? Are you nuts?" Coach Dooley said he'd be willing to wait until tomorrow, but that was it. "If you don't want this job, I've got to move on, and I've got to move quick."

I knew what accepting the job would mean, the toll it would take on my family, on my health, on everything else. I'd seen the pressure that comes with that position. And though I wanted it, it still scared me. Does that make sense?

Katharyn knew her Bible, though—how 2 Timothy 1:7 (NKJV) says, "God has not given us a spirit of fear." She said, "Mark, this fear is not coming from God. It's coming from somewhere else. Don't listen to it." I knew she was right. I knew I was just letting myself get carried away. But that's what fear does, you know. It distorts the truth. It shifts all your attention to the costs, shifts it away from the opportunity. More importantly, like I said before, it fights against your faith. It fights against the kind of heart and trust that God is working to cultivate in us. We're supposed to "walk by faith, not by sight" (2 Cor. 5:7). That's the difference that being a Christian makes.

By later that night, I was starting to feel better about everything—that is, until I told our ten-year-old son, Jon, what I was probably going to do. I remember him crying on his bed, like his whole world was about to end. He didn't want to leave. And I understood that. It's hard on kids to uproot them from familiarity. "But, son," I said, "you can be right down there on the sideline with me. You can hold the cords for my headset." He seemed to like the sound of that.

After wrestling with the decision till about 2:00 or 3:00 in the morning, I finally made up my mind. I was taking it.

Then I got concerned that I'd waited too late.

I picked up the phone right then—yes, middle of the night— and dialed Coach Dooley's number. "Coach, it's Mark Richt," I said, "I want the job."

"Uh, good," he said. "That's wonderful. But why are you calling me in the middle of the night?"

"I'm sorry, Coach, I was afraid you might sleep on it and change your mind, so I wanted to catch you before you woke up."

I never get tired of remembering that story. I was about to have *another* great man that I loved working for.

═══

One of the features I brought along with me from Florida State was a Coach Bowden creation known as "mat drills." We did them my first offseason at Georgia in 2001; we did them my last offseason at Georgia in 2015; we did them every year in between. And, trust me, not a single player who ever endured them has ever forgotten them.

The premise is simple. There's nothing new or special or scientific about it. They're really just a series of conditioning drills that have been around forever. Pretty routine stuff. But the *way* Coach Bowden did them, and the way we did them at Georgia (and later at Miami) is what made them different.

Imagine it's February. Imagine it's about 5:00 in the morning. It's chilly and dark when you arrive at the gym. Everybody's dressed in matching T-shirts and shorts. The whole team sits down on a huge wrestling mat at the center of the room—or *most* of the team anyway, as many as would fit. The rest sit behind them or around them on the gym floor, everyone in perfectly straight rows and perfectly straight columns, with legs crossed and elbows on knees. Military style.

After a brief time of announcements and warm-ups, you break into three groups: *big* (offensive and defensive linemen); *big skill* (tight ends, fullbacks, and linebackers); and *skill* (QBs, DBs, running backs, receivers). Each group disperses to one of three stations, where they spend twenty non-stop minutes on a series of related drills before rotating to the next station.

One is the form-running station, where you work on movement, core strength, and proper body position. Another is the agility station, consisting of three different drills: ropes, three-man shuttle, and the "pens," where you perform drills while bent underneath a structure of low-hanging, canvas tarps. No standing up to relieve the screaming muscles in your knees, thighs, and abs.

But the toughest of all, both physically and mentally, as well as the toughest in terms of accountability, are the drills run at the mat station. That's why we called the whole program *mat drills.*

The "two-point wave," for instance. (The two "points" would be your two feet, not to be confused with the "four-point wave," which is done on all fours. We had *many* kinds of wave drills.) Players step up to the mat in lines of four or five across. The coach assigned to that location calls out, "Ready!" All five guys jump from the floor to the mat, assuming a taut football position: knees bent, flat back, chest up, eyes up.

"Feet!" the coach shouts. Each player starts chopping his feet up and down, pumping like a piston, as quick and fast as he can do it.

Then, "Go!" They dive flat out on their chests, spread-eagle to the mat, then pop back up and resume a football position, feet buzzing away like before. Left! Right! Forward! Back! Then

"Slam!" They drop to their chest again, pop back up, then sprint full-speed—always full-speed—to the edge of the mat.

But it's not over yet. Every drill had a finish line, a set of cones positioned at the end of each station. Sometimes there might be only one more step between the orange cone at the end and a padded wall, but you hit the cone at a full sprint anyway. Boom!

And so with feet still buzzing at the edge of the mat, they wait for the coach who's stationed there to give them a "Go!" command, initiating a final sprint to the cones, followed by a thumbs-up or thumbs-down. *Up,* you're done with that drill. *Down,* everybody goes back and starts over. *Do it again.*

Wave after wave of players come through. The first group's "Go!" is the next group's "Ready!" And if one guy—just one guy— makes a mistake or is dogging it, the whole group goes back and does it again. If one fails, you all fail.

Do it right, do it hard, or do it again.

For a solid hour. Twenty minutes per station. Across all three stations. Without a single stop.

And at every place on the floor, every coach is challenging you: finish every drill.

Finish The Drill!

That was our mantra. That was the purpose of mat drills.

Well, there were a lot of purposes really. *Teamwork.* Everybody's day depended on everybody else's. You had to work together, work for your brother, or else every other guy in your group suffered the consequences of your failure. *Attention to detail.* Little things. Precise movements. Flawless technique. No room for carelessness or sloppiness. That's how you win ball games, not to mention how you win at life—by doing the little things and doing them right. *Mental toughness.* Equally important as being physically precise was becoming mentally sharp, demanding your own best, pushing past the limits of your pain.

But above all, *finish*! Don't quit. Don't pull up when things get tough. Fight through it. Finish stronger than you started. When you're tired, when you're hurting, when you're dying inside, still sprint to that cone. For your team. For your mission. For your coaches. For yourself.

Finish.

The Drill.

It was a challenge, man. It was the toughest thing we did. In fact, as an assistant at Florida State, as one of the guys who was out in the middle of all that, blowing whistles and giving the thumbs-up or thumbs-down, I'll be honest with you, I was like, "Is this really necessary? Should we be putting these guys through all this?" Because it was hell. But I became a believer in it, especially once I became a head coach. I realized mat drills were necessary to establish our leadership and our standards of work ethic.

The reason I mention "leadership" is because after every day the coaches got together to grade every player on every drill, then posted the grades for everyone to see. On the first day of mat drills each year, the lines of five were formed in order of seniority, from upper classmen to freshmen. But on each day following, the lines were formed in order of daily grades. And, trust me, you wanted to be one of the leaders. You wanted to be on a line with your highest performing teammates. That was your best shot at surviving, because as many as ten guys had to do it right, or you had to go back and do it again. So you wanted to be surrounded by people whose mental and physical motor was strong and reliable, like yours. It helped define who our true leaders were.

Mat drills were a rite of passage. A badge of honor. To not quit took everything you had. Not everybody made it. And the ones who didn't were off the team. So, the stakes were high.

But if you could survive mat drills, you were on your way to becoming a man.

That's probably why every year that I coached, whenever I'd bump into a former player at an airport or ball game or somewhere, one of the first things they'd ask me was, "Hey, Coach, you still doing mat drills?" You bet we were. Because if we weren't, they would've told me I was going soft. But I didn't get into coaching to teach guys that it doesn't matter how hard you work, how long you persevere, or how well you finish.

Finish the drill. Otherwise, there's no point in starting.

Finish the drill. Otherwise, there's no point in starting.

———

Our first, biggest test of the year during my first season at Georgia—after the entire country had been tested by the unprecedented tragedies of September 11—came October 6 on the road against #6 Tennessee. Coach Phillip Fulmer's team, in his tenth season at his alma mater, would flirt again with the national championship. If not for losing to LSU in the SEC title game, they'd have been in the big game again.

Not only was Tennessee good *that* year, but they had dominated recent history in the Georgia series. Before an upset loss in Athens the previous year—which had been unexpected enough to Bulldog fans and students that they'd rushed the field and torn down the goalposts at Sanford Stadium—the Vols had won the last nine meetings in a row. It had actually been *twenty* years since Georgia had beaten UT in Knoxville (not since Herschel Walker was a freshman, just to give you a frame of reference).

So here we go—my first away game as an SEC coach, in front of 107,000 mostly orange-clad fans at Neyland Stadium. They pulled out in front of us early, but the score was tied 17–all heading into the fourth quarter. A field goal put us up by three, but Casey Clausen moved them into our territory, driving late. Just as it looked like they were going to score to pull ahead, our Jermaine Phillips picked off a pass at the 25, giving us the ball with under two minutes to go. Was it over?

No. We failed to get a first down, and Tennessee had all three time-outs to burn. We took only nineteen seconds off the clock in three plays. After a booming punt, they had a minute and a half to pull off a comeback, starting just outside their own 20.

But, oh—gut punch. Just a few plays in, Clausen tossed a screen pass to running back Travis Stephens, who threaded through our zone coverage, accelerated along the left sideline, and was dragged down at the pylon on a sixty-two-yard scoring play.

They led 24–20.

Fifty-seven seconds to go.

Neyland Stadium was literally shaking. The *ground* was shaking beneath your feet. From where I was standing on the visitor's sidelines, you could feel the tremors disorienting your body. It was pandemonium.

They squibbed the kick, trying to prevent a big return. Probably a mistake. It allowed us to start at the 40. Red-shirt freshman David Greene, picking up bits of yardage wherever he could find it, eventually linked up with tight end Randy McMichael on two huge completions, putting the ball on the 6 with only ten seconds to play.

Time-out. It was so loud on the sideline that I was having to yell at close range, directly into the earhole of David's helmet.

I was telling him to run "P44 Haynes."

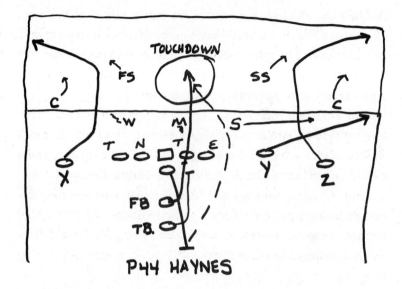

P44 HAYNES

"P" meant play-action pass. "44" was the running play we were faking. And "Haynes" was the name of our fullback, Verron Haynes. He was the one that the play was designed to feature. When we ran this same play at Florida State, P44 Haynes might be P44 Joey, the nickname of our fullback Dan Kendra, or whoever else was fullback that particular year.

P44 Haynes. It might work. Or it might not. That's what I was hollering into David's ear, explaining to him. "Look, if it's split-safety, it's gonna be there." If Tennessee lined up with two safeties, they'd most likely bracket the outside receivers and leave the middle open, with only a linebacker staying in to protect that part of the field. "But if it's one-high safety, they're probably in man-to-man. Just throw it away. We'll still have time to run another play."

David Greene was awesome. David Greene *listened* like few other guys I ever coached. He was crisp and precise and followed instructions down to the most minute detail. I knew, when he got out there, he would see what to do.

So with ten seconds left, we line up in the I, with Verron Haynes at fullback. Verron, a senior from the Bronx, had been in my doghouse earlier in the year. I'd had to suspend him from the first game. He didn't like that very much. But he'd fought back and become a team captain. And he was about to take a giant leap into Georgia legend.

We faked the run, with Verron blasting toward the Mike (middle) linebacker, as if to block him, forcing him to come up and look for the ball carrier. But instead of blocking, Verron blew past the linebacker and ran right into the end zone. David, a lefty, faked the handoff to his right, then twisted his body and floated the ball over the line to Verron, who was waiting all alone.

Touchdown.

It inspired one of the most classic radio calls of all time from iconic Georgia broadcaster Larry Munson:

> Did you see what he did? David Greene just straightened up, and we snuck the fullback over! We just dumped it over! 26–24! We just stepped on their face with a hobnail boot and broke their nose! We just crushed their face!

Wild celebration in the locker room. Here was this first-time coach, this nobody, who most people had never heard of, and all of a sudden it looked like my coaching staff and I might know a little something about what we were doing. That game gave us our first big dose of street cred. Much more importantly, of course, it was sweet reward for our players who had worked and hustled and proven their dedication to our football team, all the way back to those dark-thirty mornings in February when they had groaned out of bed and gutted out another cycle around the mats.

In fact, after I managed to get the room semi-quiet and had the players' and coaches' attention just long enough to say, "Men,

I'm so proud of you," somebody in that sea of Bulldog jerseys—I don't remember who—yelled out, "Coach! We finished the drill!"

That's right. We finished the drill.

Now it was *our* turn to shake the house.

———

Some teams adopt a different slogan or motto to rally around each season. For us, at Georgia, we had the same one every year. And it all started that day, after that game, when refusing to quit led to one of the great victories in Bulldog history.

"Finish the drill!"

It went on our walls. It went on our T-shirts. It went out into the public, among our fans. Because it's more than just a football lesson; it's a life lesson. It's more than just not quitting on a sports field. It's not quitting on your relationships. Not quitting on your marriage. Not quitting academically or on your job. Not quitting when you're going through a hard time.

> It's more than just a football lesson; it's a life lesson. It's more than just not quitting on a sports field.

I can't tell you how often through the years at Georgia, people would write and ask me to say something encouraging to one of their loved ones who was in the middle of a challenge or crisis, maybe a person who was undergoing cancer treatments or something. I'd say to them nearly every time, "On our team we talk about finishing the drill." I'd encourage them to keep believing, keep hoping, keep working as hard as they could. Then routinely I'd hear how that person decided to make it *their* little mantra as well. "I'm not gonna quit. I'm gonna be like a Bulldog. I'm gonna finish the drill."

Several years ago, Verron Haynes called me up on the phone, completely out of the blue. That's why I've kept my same cell phone number that I had in Athens, so that former players can always know how to reach me. He was telling me about his daughter. "She's in a dance class," he said, "and she hates it. She's been wanting to quit. But I said to her, hey, 'the Haynes family, we don't quit. We finish the drill.'"

A few years later, I heard from him again. After playing several years in the NFL, Verron had gone back to finish the last couple of courses he lacked from earning his college degree. Though it had been more than ten years since he last stepped foot in a classroom, he braved the challenge of going back to school and completing what he started.

At his graduation ceremony, his son came up to him, looked him in the eye, and repeated back to him the same words Verron had been pounding into his kids' heads for as long as they could remember. "Dad, you finished the drill."

Yeah.

Whatever you do, finish the drill.

11

When Leaders Lead

Why do some people avoid leadership?

I've got a few thoughts on that.

Reason 1: *They don't feel like they're worthy.* Go back with me to that lonely hotel room after I'd become the head coach at Georgia, when I was flat on my face, crying out to God, telling him (like Moses did) that I didn't think I was capable of doing this job. Believing you're not up to what God has called you to do and has gifted you to do, even with the promise of His help and guidance, is a major obstacle to becoming the leader you're meant to be.

Reason 2: *They're afraid to fail.* That was my problem at East Carolina. I was so worried about not being able to lead an offense that, guess what?—I wasn't leading the offense. I was allowing myself to be intimidated by fear of failure instead of humbly, yet confidently, trusting God to shape me into the kind of leader He'd made me to be, even if it was different from the type of leader He'd made others to be. If you're trying to emulate somebody else, it'll never work. You can't lead like that. I was afraid my way would fail, but in reality my way was the best way because it was true to who I really was. You've gotta be you. Leaders aren't afraid to be themselves.

But there's at least one other reason why people avoid leadership.

Reason 3: *It's not popular.*

I suppose the most universal example is in the role of parenting. Parenting is leadership. But the decisions made by parents are not always popular. A mom or dad says to one of their kids, "I want you home at 10:00 tonight," even when all their friends, they say, get to stay out till midnight. So what? You've made a decision that you believe is in the best interest of your child. Are you going to back away from that, away from *leading*, just because it's not winning you any parent-points at the moment?

See, all of us are leaders. If you have influence over anybody in your life, you're a leader. Even if it's just by your everyday example, where the people you know are watching you and noticing how you live and conduct yourself, you can't say, "No, I'm not a leader." Yes, you are. What you're really saying is you don't feel *worthy* of being a leader, or you're afraid you'd *fail* if you tried to be a leader, or you're not willing to risk being *unpopular* to be a leader. And yet the opportunity is there—to lead in your life right now—if you'll just take ownership of the responsibility and step into it.

The same thing happens on a football team. Leaders become leaders by leading when it's not popular, when they have the guts to say things or do things that the players around them don't want to hear or see.

An unforgettable example happened in my second year at Georgia, at halftime of a late-season game against Auburn. We came into that week playing good ball, a continuation of the year prior where we'd finished 8-4. It had been the first time in school history that a first-year coach had won eight ball games. By the Auburn game in year two—the next-to-last game on our 2002 schedule before the annual closer against Georgia

Tech—we were 9-1 (6-1 in conference), our only loss against Florida in Jacksonville. A win at Auburn would put us in the SEC championship game—again, first time in Georgia history since the conference championship match was instituted in 1992.

I attribute a lot of our early success to the "win now" mentality we brought into the program as a coaching staff. We told the seniors, from the minute we got there, that we hadn't come to Georgia with a three-year plan for building a championship-caliber team with "our guys," the players we were in the process of recruiting for future seasons. As soon as we walked into that locker room in the 2001 offseason, "our guys" were the players who were already on that team—which, by the way, included a lot of really great players. The previous staff had recruited extremely well. They definitely hadn't left the cupboard bare. Still, the only way we were going to have success right now, we told them, was if the seniors and other leaders from the previous regime immediately bought in. The reason they could commit to *us* was because we were committed to *them*.

In 2002, our team was senior-laden, containing an impressive number of gifted leaders. So in order to make the most of that asset, and in order to encourage them to grow personally in their leadership abilities, I kicked off our team meetings that year with some teaching from John Maxwell's *The 21 Most Powerful Minutes in a Leader's Day*. A gentleman named Bobby Lankford had given me that book early in my career at Georgia, and I was repeatedly amazed at how often it hit the nail directly on the head regarding the kinds of things I was dealing with on a daily basis. It was instrumental in helping me keep developing as a leader myself.

One of John's leadership "laws" that I emphasized with the team that year was what he calls "The Law of the Lid." Basically, he says a team (or company or office or family) will only perform up to the level that its leadership will take it. If you put a lid on the leadership, you put a lid on the whole program. Take the lid off, however, and the sky's the limit.

We'd seen this principle bear fruit with that 2002 team. Things were jelling. Guys were believing. We were on the precipice of the first 11-win season since some of Coach Dooley's teams from the 1970s and early '80s. But we needed to take care of business on the road at Auburn on November 16. And by halftime, that wasn't happening. We were losing 14–3.

Halftime in a college locker room is fairly programmed. While the players are changing their shirts or going to the bathroom or whatever, the coaches are getting together in their groups—offense, defense, special teams—discussing any adjustments they need to make in the second half. As head coach, I would circulate among them, finding out what they needed me to say when I addressed the team before we headed back out onto the field.

So as I'm off in an adjacent room pulling my notes together before giving my halftime speech that day, I hear yelling coming from the big room where the players were gathered. Not *many* voices, like a fight. *One* voice, like a butt-chewing. And cocking my head to listen, I could tell it was the voice of Jon Stinchcomb, our fifth-year senior, starting offensive tackle, reaming out his teammates, himself included.

Jon was a high achiever, a 4.0, straight-A student who was excellent in everything he did. In mat drills, for example— remember "mat drills" from the last chapter?—Jon's first posted grade was a C-plus, which was probably one of the higher grades on the team, but still it wasn't a letter he was accustomed to seeing on his report card. I remember him coming to me, saying, "Coach, I've never gotten a C on anything in my life," kind of pleading his case to me. I said, "Jon, if you want a better grade, just do a better job." And he did. That's who he was. A worker. A winner. A leader.

That's why I wasn't surprised to hear him leading at that moment at halftime of the Auburn game. "I didn't come to Georgia to lose!" he was screaming. "I came to be a champion! We worked too hard to get here, and we're letting each other down!" He was calling his teammates *and* himself up to the level of play they were capable of giving. In language I can't repeat, he was rallying every man in a Bulldog uniform that day to a better effort than they'd put out in the first thirty minutes. Again, himself included. He wasn't trying to be popular; he was demanding a positive change to the outcome of that game and to the rest of our season.

He was leading.

The television announcers, after we'd come out with a strong opening drive to start the second half, were saying, you know, "Mark Richt is not an overly emotional guy, but he must have ripped 'em one good at halftime, because they're playing like the seventh-ranked team in the country now." No, it wasn't that way at all. The truth is, I stepped out into the locker room, stood quietly for a second, and said, "I've got nothing left to say. *He said* it," pointing to Stinchcomb. "Let's go."

Sure enough, we did execute a solid, ten-play touchdown drive right out of the gate to make a game of it. Then in fitting style, Stinchcomb recovered a fumble in the Auburn end zone late in the third for another touchdown. But with 1:58 to play, we started our last drive of the game after returning an Auburn punt, which put us in decent field position at our 41, but at a 21–17 deficit. After moving inside the 20 on a long pass from David Greene to our go-to receiver, Fred Gibson, we stalled with a series of incompletions and a motion penalty, making it fourth and fifteen.

Unlike the Tennessee game, we had no time-outs to use, no way to give detailed instructions to Greene about how to handle the final play call. To complicate matters even further, I decided to go with a play—70X Take-Off—that we hadn't practiced in weeks. We'd installed it early in the season, but we hadn't run it in a while. And I'll admit, that's unusual—running a play at a critical moment in the game that nobody's thought about for a month.

Here was my logic in choosing it. Michael Johnson, one of our wide receivers, had been having a career day. He'd caught twelve balls for more than a hundred yards, by far his most productive game ever in a Georgia uniform. But Fred Gibson, though compromised a little that day by a thumb injury, was still our big-stud pass-catcher. Auburn would be expecting us to target him.

On "70X Take-Off," which looks like this . . .

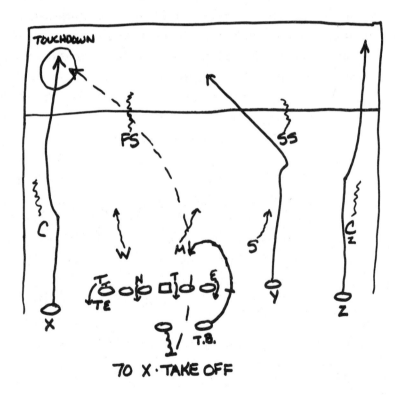

70 X · TAKE OFF

. . . Michael was lined up as the X, split to the left; Mario Raley was the Y, the slot receiver; Fred, the Z, was at the far right. All three guys "take off" for the end zone. But because it's 70X Take-Off, the play was designed to go to Michael. Greene's job, in order to sell it and make it work, was to pump toward Gibson streaking down the right sideline, luring the back-side safety to cheat that direction, then turn and fire to Johnson, who should be one-on-one with his defender. But again, it all depended on the quarterback's long-term memory and his instant grasp of what to do the minute he heard the play call.

With David, I was willing to take that chance. He was just machine-like in his study habits and preparedness. The reason he became a four-year starter, closing his career with more wins at quarterback than anyone else in college football history at the time, was because he never had one of those outings where you wanted to yank him. His play never cost us a game. He was steadily consistent, a special player.

And that Saturday afternoon at Auburn was just another example of it. To hear Larry Munson tell it . . .

> We're on the 19, we've got to get to the 4 for the first down. The crowd roars at us. Three wide-outs. Man, we've had some shots, haven't we? Snap to David Greene, there he goes in the corner again, and we jump up—*touchdown!* . . . a touchdown! In the corner! With eighty-five seconds! Somebody went up high. Was it Watson or Gibson? Michael Johnson up high. We're gonna put glasses on it . . . Michael Johnson turned around and got up into the air. We caught the ball! 23–21, with eighty-five seconds!

Exciting.

I'm pumped all over again.

But I think it's fair to say, this play and this moment was made possible, more than anything, by an offensive lineman—a leader—who dared to challenge his teammates at halftime, down in the bowels of a hostile stadium, making the unpopular choice to go vocal with the effort he saw lacking in both his own and his team's performance.

The announcers had been right. We came out looking like a different unit.

That's the difference leaders make.

=====

Speaking of Jon Stinchcomb, it's worth mentioning another player on that Georgia team who exemplified the quality of leading when it's not popular. David Pollack was probably the most relentless player I've ever been around. A three-time All-American. To put it in perspective, the only other three-time All-American in the history of Georgia football was Herschel Walker.

David Pollack belongs in that echelon. A Lombardi Award winner, first-round draft pick, and now a member of the College Football Hall of Fame, he made himself popularly unpopular by the tenacity of his work ethic. His teammates loved him. When they weren't hating him.

Stinchcomb, for instance. I think he and Pollack got into a fight every day in practice.

David was recruited as a fullback, but was moved to the interior defensive line as a freshman, like at noseguard. He was kind of chubby at the time, but he worked extremely hard. Heading into his sophomore year, we'd lost three defensive ends—two by graduation, one by declaring early for the draft—leaving us thin on the outside. Our defensive staff thought David would make a good candidate for shifting over into that slot. We at least knew he'd go hard at it. He wasn't really the prototypical defensive end, from a physical standpoint. He was a little too heavy. But we knew he'd give maximum effort.

By the time we made the switch during the offseason, he didn't have time to get his body right for playing a new position. All spring long, lined up against Stinchcomb, he was getting whipped play after play. They really did fight just about every day, no kidding. But he was tenacious. He knew he needed to get quicker; he knew he needed to drop weight; or else he knew he'd keep getting his butt kicked, not only in practice but in games. So by the end of spring ball to the beginning of the season, that's when the transformation kicked in. He worked with Jon Fabris, our defensive ends coach, who was meticulous about technique and detail, and David brought the same intensity to his own preparation that he brought to every single practice.

Pollack was the rare kind of guy who, even as a freshman, didn't care if he was irritating the veterans. He'd run those sprints and gassers at top speed in the summer, even when older guys were saying, "Slow down, rookie." It just didn't faze him. He wasn't there to make friends, to be popular. He was there to be great.

And he did it. He became great. He set the school record for sacks that very year, his first year at the position—went from being a pudgy backup noseguard to one of the best defensive ends in America, all in one season.

I'll bet if you're a Georgia fan, you remember the day he drew the nation's eye for the first real time.

It actually occurred earlier in this same 2002 season, second game of the year, on the road at South Carolina. Both teams pretty much stunk it up on offense the entire game. We led only 3–0 going into the fourth quarter. After another stalled drive in a whole day's worth of stalled drives, we pinned the Gamecocks inside their 5 on a terrific pooch punt by Jonathan Kilgo. Then on second and eight, quarterback Corey Jenkins faded back to pass, a couple of steps into the end zone. Pollack brought pressure off the edge, lunging just as Jenkins brought his arm forward. But somehow in the process of getting his left hand up to bat down the pass, he carried the ball with him all the way to the ground. The quarterback didn't even know where it went. I'm not sure David even knew where it went. But when the play was over, he was down on his knees in the end zone with the ball tucked inside his left elbow. Technically an interception. Definitely a touchdown. Absolutely his last day as an anonymous football player.

The sideline reporter, at the conclusion of the game, asked me, "How about that 'Po-lock' interception in the end zone?"

I corrected her. "It's David *PAH-luck*," I said, "and I think after today, people are gonna learn how to say his name and they're gonna know what kind of ballplayer he is."

They sure would.

The kind of ballplayer, the kind of leader, who leads others even when it's not popular.

12

The Hot Seat

One of our coaches, having decided to make what seemed, to me, a lateral move to join another coaching staff, asked if I would give him one last opportunity to address the players on his side of the ball before he left. Being a young head coach, I thought that was fine, but I said I wanted to be in the room as well.

I'm not saying he didn't mean the words he spoke to those players that day—how he loved them, how much he'd enjoyed coaching them, how he knew they were each poised to do great things on the football field if they continued to work hard and make the proper sacrifices. All I know is that, as I took the measure of the room, I could sense the hurt that many of them were feeling. You could see it in their countenance, in their body language. *Oh, great. Another guy, walking out on me. More change. More stress.* That's the vibe I was picking up.

So after the coach had said his piece, I told him I was going to stay behind and speak to the players in private. As soon as we were alone, just the players and me, I said to them, "I want you to know one thing. *I'm* not going anywhere. I'm staying right here. And I promise you, I will go out and get for you the best coach I can find, a guy who'll come in here and take care of you."

Loyalty matters.

I'm going to sound a little old-school here, I know, but it saddens me to see the painful consequences of disloyalty in our world today. People who didn't keep their promises. People who believed that their own concerns and desires were more important than anybody else's. People who let circumstances, not convictions, determine their decisions. People who chose individual goals over team goals.

I've mentioned this before, but God has blessed me with several up-close, powerful examples of long-term loyalty in my life. Coach Bowden would be near the top—the commitment he made to his faith, his team, and his family over decades and decades. I'd seen his loyalty result in success, for everybody involved, again and again.

Here's just one example. When Chris Weinke made the decision in preseason camp to declare for the 1990 baseball draft, Coach said to him as he was leaving, "If you ever want to come back, you'll always have a scholarship at Florida State." Six or seven years passed. We continued to go after and sign highly touted quarterbacks: Danny Kanell, Thad Busby, Kenny Felder (who, like Chris, also ended up going the pro baseball route), among others.

One of those signees was Dan Kendra III, who not only had been tabbed as the national high school player of the year by several top publications and recruiting services, but he was also son of the Dan Kendra who'd been one of Coach Bowden's quarterbacks at West Virginia. Dan, in fact, (or "Joey," as we called him, because that's what he called everybody else) was born while his dad was still playing ball at WVU. And Ann Bowden, Coach's wife, had written a note at the time to go along with his baby gift, addressing it, "To our future quarterback." Sure enough, by 1997, he was Florida State's quarterback in waiting.

Still, early that year, Coach Bowden stepped into my office and said, "Mark, guess what? Do you remember old Weinke?"

"Sure."

"Well, he doesn't want to play baseball anymore. He wants to play football."

"He's coming back?"

"Yeah. I promised him he could."

"But, Coach—"

As much as it sounded like good news to him, and as much as it might ordinarily have sounded like good news to me, having Kendra and now Weinke on the same roster would spoil all the work we'd done to sign a kid named Drew Henson to a letter-of-intent. I believed we were right on the verge of securing him—one of the top QBs in the country, who would go on to unseat a guy named Tom Brady as the starter at Michigan. Weinke's unexpected arrival was sure to scare Henson and his parents away.

So I asked Coach Bowden if I could talk to Chris myself before word got out. We'd had him in camp, remember, before he opted for baseball, so I'd worked with him briefly as quarterbacks coach years before. We had enough of a relationship for me to call him on the phone and say, "Hey, I hear you're wanting to come back."

"Yes, sir, I am."

"Well, that's great, Chris, but . . . you do need to understand something. Number one: I know you're a grown man now. You've got money. You're accustomed to doing what you want to do. But I've got a bunch of eighteen- to twenty-two-year-olds here, and we've gotta do things a certain way, or else it won't work. You're gonna have to do what everybody else is expected to do."

"Of course, Coach. No problem."

"Okay." Looked like my first approach hadn't worked. As crazy as it sounds now, I was literally trying to talk him out of this.

"Here's the other thing," I said. "We've got this Dan Kendra kid." I then went on to tell him about the Kendra family's history with Coach Bowden. "Dan's the national player of the year," I added, knowing the clout of that title would register with Weinke. He'd been prep player of the year himself coming out of high school in Minnesota. But that was seven years ago. Did he still have the football skills to go up against the level of competition he'd be facing now? Even the in-house competition?

"Coach," he said, in typical Weinke fashion, "answer me one question. If I'm the best player, will I start?"

How else could I answer that? "Yes," I said.

"Okay. Then I'm coming."

As it turned out, Kendra ended up getting hurt in preseason practice. He would come back the next year and play well for us at fullback, which probably fit his body type better anyway. But Weinke was there to step in and lead us to a national championship, and eventually play himself into winning the Heisman Trophy. Coach Bowden's loyalty to keep his promises had paid off, as it usually does.

Loyalty matters.

I'd include Coach Dooley, too, in that select group of men in my life who've exemplified loyalty. He coached at Georgia for twenty-five years. Most of those teams in most of those years were highly successful. Only one losing season in that entire run. He coached until 1988, doubling as the athletic director beginning in 1979, and continued serving as AD while I was there until his retirement in 2004. Fierce loyalty.

Some people told me, before I even went there, "You don't want to take that Georgia job, Mark. Coach Dooley will be in your hair the whole time, telling you how to run the program." I was, like, "Isn't he one of the greatest coaches of all time? I think I'd *like* Coach Dooley to be in my business."

But he never intruded in that way. He stayed in those upper floors of the building and would rarely come down where our football offices were—not because he was disinterested but because he didn't want to put undue pressure on me. I would go to *him* quite often to talk about issues that came up. His door was always open. But even then, most of our conversations were about off-the-field matters, not game micro-management.

I can think of only one time that he offered me any specific coaching advice. It was after a game where we'd botched our special-teams coverage on a punt return by not sending even one guy to put pressure on the punter, which ended up looking particularly bad because of the way the play ended up. The snap had been poor, the punter dropped the ball, fumbled around with it for a while, yet was still able to get the kick away easily because we'd dropped everybody back. (Coach was a hundred percent right, of course.)

I loved having him as athletic director because he'd been a football coach himself. He knew exactly what I was dealing with. He understood that I'd have some players who misbehaved and would need to be disciplined. None of that surprised him or caused him to overreact. His general line of counsel toward me was to do what I thought was best, to trust my own judgment, not to worry about what other people thought if I had solid reasons for making hiring choices or disciplinary choices or whatever other kinds of choices I was faced with. Those "crisis per week" choices that Coach Bowden had warned me about.

Coach Dooley was loyal to me. He was wonderful to me, to us. Still is. Katharyn and I love him and his wife, Barbara. He's another man who's proven to me the priceless importance of loyalty to a school, to a team, to the people you care about.

═══

We borrowed a number of successful team-building practices at Georgia from Coach Bowden's years at Florida State. The annual *Hideaway* meeting at the start of the football year, for example. *Mat drills* that tormented our players while building their character. But at least one team-building exercise was completely original to our coaching staff.

The "Hot Seat."

We were recruiting a kid, DeMario Minter, a defensive back out of Stone Mountain, Georgia. Among my memories of visiting in his family's home was an interesting dinner combination of lasagna and fried turkey. It was . . . it was glorious. I'd say it ranked top-five all-time in-home visits, in terms of quality of the food. (And don't think we didn't keep rankings of such things.) Willie Martinez, our secondary coach, was there with me that night, I remember, along with Rodney Garner, our recruiting coordinator. They'd back me up on that.

But as we moved into the family living room, after enjoying that outrageously delicious meal, DeMario's grandfather took over the conversation. They had one of those sectional couches that featured a recliner in the middle, right where the two sofas met. This seat, we were told, was the grandfather's seat. Everybody knew not to sit there. But he was making a temporary exception during this period while his grandson was being recruited by various schools to play football. "This is my chair normally," he said, "but tonight it's the 'hot seat.' I want you to sit in that chair, Coach Richt," he said to me, "and tell us why my grandson should go to Georgia."

As I got up and began moving toward the "hot seat," trying to think of what I was going to say, DeMario's grandfather continued laying out the ground rules. "You have the floor. Everyone will listen to you. No one will interrupt you. Speak whatever you want, just speak it from your heart." So I settled in. And I guess I must have done okay. DeMario did come to Georgia, earned first-team all-SEC honors in 2005, and became a fifth-round NFL draft pick.

But perhaps in some ways his most lasting imprint on the University of Georgia football program, during my tenure there at least, was the implementation of the Hot Seat.

Here's how it worked. After dinner each evening during preseason camp, all the players and coaches would gather in the team meeting room. It was one of those rooms with tiered seating that funneled down toward a main presentation area in the front. That's where we set up a chair, right in the center, and designated it the Hot Seat. Any player who wanted, we told them, could get up, come down there, and say whatever he felt like saying, describing in his own words what it meant to be a Bulldog. We encouraged the seniors to go first, to take the lead in sharing their thoughts, but anyone could have their moment. The same rules applied as DeMario's grandfather had laid down: Everybody listens. No one interrupts. Speak your mind. Speak your heart.

The only other rule that applied—and this is why it worked so well—is that whatever was said in that room *stayed* in that room. Guys could say anything they wanted to say and could be sure it would remain private. That's why even before writing up the couple of Hot Seat moments that I'm about to share with you in this chapter, I asked both players specifically for their permission. This many years later, I still don't want to break the code. That's how highly I value my loyalty to *them*.

Boss Bailey, for example, I recall—our outstanding, All-American linebacker, younger brother of Champ Bailey—said from the Hot Seat one night, "Coach Richt came in here and showed us a film of Peter Warrick and Laveranues Coles doing mat drills, all smiling and happy, tearing it up. We thought it was gonna be something great. Might even be fun. And now it's, like, the worst thing we've ever done in our lives. I was thinking, 'Dang, man, we should've played harder for Coach Donnan. We wouldn't have to be doing this crap right now.'"

Mat drills. Don't get 'em started on that.

But probably my most enduring memory of the Hot Seat was the night in 2005 when senior quarterback D. J. Shockley took his place there. Shock was the first player to commit to Georgia after I became head coach. I'd actually recruited him at Florida State when I was offensive coordinator there, so getting him to say yes was a great personal victory.

And he was a great player. But it just so happened, as it sometimes does, that his college career overlapped with that of another great player, David Greene. As a coach, you can never have too many good players. But that's not always the case when you're one of the good players yourself.

D. J. came out of Atlanta as the #2-rated dual-threat quarterback in America, and yet he was #2 on the depth chart for his own team. That's tough to take. Many, including himself, including his own father (who happened to have been his high school football coach), weren't sure he should hang around for that. Big-name programs were interested in his services, the moment he decided he'd been carrying the clipboard long enough.

As I recall, he was the first to take the seat that evening—the all-everything quarterback who'd waited four years to be the starting quarterback. He said, "Fellas, a lot of people thought I should leave. Nothing against Greene, you know, because he was great. Everybody knew that. But I knew I wasn't going to play much with him being here. People always kept asking me, 'Why don't you leave?'

"Two reasons: Number one is because of my twin brothers. They both have Fragile-X syndrome [a genetic disorder that causes learning disabilities]. But they are Bulldogs through and through. And they just wouldn't understand—it would break their hearts—if I'd have told them I was going somewhere else.

"That's number one. But here's number two," he said, beginning to raise his arm, sweeping it to one side, then to the other, pointing his finger at player after player. "It's because of every man in this room."

Because of team. Because of loyalty.

Those guys would've done *anything* for him after that. (Probably before that, too, but certainly after it.)

If you asked him about it today, he'd tell you there was also a number three. He'd tell you how he'd come into my office a couple of years earlier, pretty sure he was going to bail on Georgia if I didn't give him some assurances about playing more. I couldn't. All I could do was be honest with him. I told him I loved him. I told him he was going to get a great education here. I didn't promise him a number of starts or a set amount of playing time. But I did make a bold, rather prophetic statement. I said, "I promise you, when you leave here, you'll go out with a smile on your face."

D. J. became the overall team captain on that 2005 group who won another SEC championship, taking down #3 LSU, 34–14, in the Georgia Dome. He was amazing that day, played just a beautiful game.

In fact, I remember sitting in my room in Atlanta the night before, watching tape. Though it's almost unheard of, I decided to add another couple of plays into the game plan that we hadn't run since early in the season. I just felt sure they would work against the defensive fronts I was seeing on film, things I hadn't noticed before. Guess what? Shock went out and turned both of them into first-quarter touchdown passes on our way to the upset victory.

He was MVP of the game that night, to go along with being selected First Team All-SEC for the season, First-Team All-Academic, and (maybe the most special and fitting of all, to me) the Bobby Bowden Athlete of the Year Award, presented by the Fellowship of Christian Athletes (FCA), bestowed on the student-athlete who epitomizes faith and excellence in the community, the classroom, and on the field. He left Georgia as a champion, was drafted, got his shot at the NFL, and today is still working in football as an on-air color commentator for ESPN.

In his house today is a picture of him and me, on the field, in the immediate aftermath of that championship victory—each of us caught in the joy of that winning moment. Along the bottom is an inscription I wrote to him: "I told you you'd leave here with a smile on your face." I'm so glad he did.

In today's college football landscape, where opting out and placing your name into the transfer portal is almost expected under certain conditions, stories like D. J. Shockley's aren't given a chance to happen a lot anymore. They don't get to inspire us often enough. He had stayed at Georgia when the pressure to leave was intense, when most of the voices in his life were advising him to look somewhere else, saying he was wasting his time and his talent by just waiting around. But in the Hot Seat, he told his teammates how to live when restlessness and discontentment is all you're feeling inside. By making the call of loyalty, you're not only setting yourself up for success, you're earning the power of influence.

By making the call of loyalty, you're not only setting yourself up for success, you're earning the power of influence.

The Bible teaches, "Never let loyalty and faithfulness leave you. Tie them around your neck; write them on the table of your heart. Then you will find favor and high regard in the sight of God and man" (Prov. 3:3–4 HCSB). Truer words never spoken.

Loyalty matters.

13

Be Prepared

Jesus primarily taught by telling stories. He knows that's how we most easily hear and understand things. Some of his stories gravitated around a similar theme: *Be prepared.*

He told a story, for example, about ten women who were waiting for a groom to show up for the man's wedding banquet. Because he was slow in arriving, the hour grew late. Five of the women hadn't brought enough oil to keep their lamps burning into the night and had to rush back into town for fresh supplies. While they were gone, the groom arrived. They'd missed him. But the five who'd thought ahead and planned for contingencies were there to welcome him, to be part of his celebration.

The point? *Be prepared.*

He told another story about a wealthy man who, before leaving on a long journey, gave money to three of his servants and instructed them to put it to good use, that he'd be expecting to see a good ROI when he got back. Two of them worked to double their money; the third man, because he was afraid to risk losing the money, held back and did nothing with his. The day came when the man returned. The two servants who'd followed their boss's orders brought proof of the profits they'd made; the other man just made excuses.

The point? A day is coming when you'll need to show your work.

Be prepared.

———

Most people watching a football game wonder how a coach decides which play to run on a particular down and distance at a particular moment in the game. They see that big oversized, laminated play card in his hand, with all that tiny writing on it, with all that multitude of options. They hear the announcers offering their opinions on what they think the right play call should be.

Even as a casual fan, maybe you sit there trying to imagine what you'd do. In your mind you know enough to see the potential downside of calling a running play, the possibility of getting stuffed at the line. You also see the downside of attempting a pass, where even *more* things need to go right for the play to be successful. Pros, cons; opportunities, obstacles.

How do you make the call?

You come prepared.

In many ways, you don't really make your call on the sideline, on Saturday. You make it in the days before, the weeks before, the months before. Before you ever get into third and seven on the 25 with three minutes left in the game, you've already been there in your head. You've prepared yourself for it.

You started going there on Sunday evening and most of Monday, when you were watching film of your upcoming opponent, jotting notes to yourself about their basic fronts and coverages.

By Tuesday, you were practicing first- and second-down plays in what's called the "green zone," the middle of the field between the 20s. Thinking in broad strokes. Sketching out your normal calls. The plays you just like. In addition, you were scheming short yardage situations. Third and one: What do they like to do on defense when the other team is only needing a yard? Third and two. Surprisingly, that's a whole different category, requiring its own line of thought. The first time it's third and two in the game, what's your favorite run, your favorite pass? Line it up against your scout team, see what you see, then put it on the call sheet. Third and one, third and two—they're all in your game plan now.

On Wednesday, you widened your third-down preferences. Third and medium (3–5 yards); third and long (6–10 yards); third and extra-long (11-plus yards). You charted those out. You know what's there for you to work with.

What about the red zone? You practiced that too. If you're between the 20 and the 10 (what we called the "high red zone"), here are your favorite plays to call. Between the 10 and the 3 (the "low red zone"), here are the ones you like. After experimenting with several others, you ranked the ones that make the most sense to you. Same thing for when you snap the ball *inside* the 3, the 2, the 1. You already know what you're likely to do in each of those scenarios.

You may wonder, "Why so much attention paid to third-down play calls?" It's because third downs are known in coach-speak as "possession downs." If you don't convert them, it most likely results in losing possession of the ball. So being prepared for how you intend to handle third downs is crucial to your game planning. Crucial to your success on game day.

Then came Thursday. More of a cleanup day. That's when you practiced your two-minute drill. You also ran your four-minute offense—those end-of-game situations where you're trying to kill the clock, where picking up two first downs probably means you win. Opposite of "red zone" situations, you worked on "black zone" situations, where you're backed up inside your own 1 or 2 or 3, where you're running the play out of your own end zone. You also spent time on two-point conversions. Except, what if your opponent hasn't faced any two-point plays this year? What if there's no available tape for that? Then you looked at how they've handled third-down situations on or near the 3-yard line, which is basically the same thing. They'll probably do something similar. You bundled it all up with everything else and put those calls into your game plan too.

After all that investment of time and work, you showed up at the game on Saturday with a series of plays you wanted to run from the first offensive snap. Even if you make a first down right off, on the first or second play, you keep rolling through your plan. Then as soon as you find yourself in, say, a third and two, guess what—you've already chosen your top plays for a third-and-two situation. You look in that square, you look at the anticipated coverage, then you look to your quarterback. You're ready to make the call.

There are times, of course, as the game plays out, when things aren't working, when the defense is doing something you weren't expecting, when you need to be able to go off-script in order to counteract it. But still, no need to panic, even if you need to revert to plays or groups of plays that you've run in games past. That's where an experienced quarterback comes in handy—like a David Greene, being prepared enough that day to know what to do when I pulled 70X Takeoff out of mothballs and into the game plan.

What I mean is, it's not like you're reduced to shooting from the hip or drawing things up in the dirt. You can trust your preparation to kick in. The fact that you've prepared well as a staff and as a team—the fact that you've done the right things the right way—means you can adjust and change things around without resorting to desperation.

So while that sheet in your hand, from the look of it on TV, appears to leave a hundred color-coded choices for a coach to sort through at any pivotal moment in the game, your preparation has already shrunk that enormous universe of options down to the size of a street corner. It's not easy, but neither is it as confusing as it looks or as complicated as it could be. *If* you're prepared.

=====

Life comes down to decisions. And most decisions, in most cases, come down to the kind of preparation you've put in. Even if something happens that you're not expecting, the seriousness of your preparation will contribute to your success in being ready for it.

Here's where I can tell you a little story about the current athletic director at the University of Georgia, Josh Brooks. When he was twenty-seven years old and working as director of football operations at Louisiana-Monroe, he heard about an opening in our program for *assistant* director of football operations, which of course was a step up the national ladder. (Although, I don't mind adding, Louisiana-Monroe had upset Alabama 21–14 the previous season, which made it a lot easier to locate ULM on the college football map.)

> Life comes down to decisions. And most decisions, in most cases, come down to the kind of preparation you've put in.

I was at my desk one day when Ann Hunt, my administrative assistant, stepped into my office with an overnight package addressed to me. "This is from a guy who's applying for the job in football ops. He wanted to be sure you saw this, in addition to his résumé and application." Opening the box, I pulled out a large binder, just filled with examples of the candidate's work—everything from camp brochures, to clinic plans, even the fine-print minutiae of how he'd organized travel itineraries, airplane seating, rooming arrangements—all neatly presented by category inside crisp dividers. It was extremely impressive.

Football operations, if you don't know, entails responsibility for just about all the logistical, operational items of the program that don't involve coaching. If you've ever wondered how a college football team gets all their people and all their stuff transported intact and on-time from their home campus to wherever they're playing a game on a fall Saturday, football operations is the right answer. They're incredible. They think of everything. Even if it's just planning a team meal or helping organize a team banquet, the football ops people are the ones who get it done. Whenever in doubt, they're the folks to call.

And Josh, from the look of things, had his fingerprints on everything at Louisiana-Monroe.

Long story short, his preparation and initiative earned him the job. He was obviously highly attentive to detail, or else he wouldn't have had all these examples of his work immediately at hand to deliver in that package. Plus, he'd put in the work to back up every piece of information he'd sent to me. When he came to Athens for an in-person interview a few days later, he was able to speak authoritatively on everything that binder represented, as well as his well-thought-out strategies for streamlining and improving this important part of the football business.

I still had other applicants to call and talk to, based on the materials they'd submitted. But it didn't take me long to know the right guy had been in my office earlier that morning. Before Josh even had time to board his plane at the Atlanta airport and head back to north Louisiana, I'd already called and offered him the job. Imagine being on the escalator at a crowded airport, no more than two or three hours removed from your late morning interview, and being offered the job before you can even get out of town.

That's what happened.

Because Josh was prepared.

Or, to put it in his words, "You don't have to *get* ready if you *stay* ready." That's probably why, little more than ten years later, he was ready for an in-house promotion to the Georgia athletic director's seat at the age of thirty-nine. Preparation keeps you ready.

The same thing went for my players. Preparation was essential. You don't really win games on the field as much as you prepare to win them in practice, in the springtime, in the classroom.

I would always tell quarterbacks, "I'm going to give you a process that'll help you make decisions under pressure," then I would drill them in it until they were sick of it. In doing so, I was helping them create good habits that would take over in the heat of battle. Ninety percent of the time, this process would put them in place to make a sound decision and run a successful play. And as for the other 10 percent of the time, I told them, they'd still be left with options: Throw the ball away? Scramble? Even just take a sack?

"Don't turn a bad play into a catastrophe," I'd tell them. If one of your blockers gets beat in protection, for example, and a defensive lineman is bearing down on you, a throwaway or a sack is no more than a bad play. We can live with that. Throwing it up for grabs, though? Risking a pick-six? That's a catastrophe. "End every drive with a kick," I'd tell them, "either an extra point, a field goal, or at worst a punt." It's all right to have a bad play; just don't have a bad day. That was my philosophy.

Every week I would test the QBs to reinforce the game plan. Page after page, each page dedicated to one of our top plays. On the test they would draw the same play against eight different fronts, coverages, and blitzes that a defense was most likely to employ against it, including how our protections were designed to hold up, as well as the various run checks that the quarterback might make from them. (*Run checks* are basically audibles where, based on the defensive formation, you either change a run play to a pass play, or you change the direction of a run from one side of the line to the other.)

As the quarterback drew the plays and the pass routes in each box, versus each of these possible looks, he would identify his job on each one. "What's my progression? Do I need to change the play? Change the protection?" All kinds of questions like that. At first it could be overwhelming, analyzing every play in eight different ways. But over time it became second nature. It engrained in them the ability to handle pressure, to make good decisions when faced with fast-moving information on the field. That "fast-moving information" is usually in the form of a 6'5", 260-pound defensive end who has bad intentions.

All the QBs, even the backups, had to go through this process. Not just nodding when I explained it. I learned from my earliest days as a quarterbacks coach that when I showed them a concept and said, "Okay? You got it?" and they nodded their heads and said, "Yeah, I got it," they didn't always have it. I needed them able to answer my direct, specific questions: "If the safety, on the snap of the ball, goes deep middle, what coverage is it?" If they'd been preparing like I'd told them, they'd know what to say to me, almost before I asked the question.

It took time, of course. It took smarts. It might even take them working together on it to figure it out. That was fine with me. As long as they were physically drawing the routes every time and noting their progressions, I knew they were learning what they needed to know. But in the end—no matter how difficult, tedious, or needless this whole testing process might seem to them—all the preparation would make a difference in their decisions. I knew that. When they got out on the field in the heat of action, their knowledge and reflexes would take over. The game, as they say, would slow down for them. They'd intuitively know what to do.

And in some ways, I think that's what all of us need to remember. More often than not, the difference between bad plays and bad days is less a function of athletic ability and more a result of preparation. The smartest guys, the most talented guys, the most naturally gifted guys—they only keep that edge over the competition for so long. The defenses figure them out, just like life figures us out. We only maintain our ability to make wise, productive choices if we're sharp in our preparation.

You and I can choose to spend our time either getting ready for what's coming up next on television or for what's coming up next in life—setting goals, planning ahead, learning from others, keeping our hearts right with God. Decisions will need to be made regardless, but they won't be made well by the careless.

Are you ready for what's coming? You *can* be.

By coming prepared.

═══

I won't say it happened only once, but I can think of one particular time in my coaching career when I sat up the night before a game, feeling like one of those people from Jesus's stories who wasn't ready for what was coming. It's not that I hadn't prepared. It's just that putting together a game plan takes a lot of creativity. And sometimes, after a while, you can get a little dry. You can be grinding, can still be doing your best, and yet you can reach that point of diminishing returns where, when you step back and analyze things under a clearer light, you're not as happy with it as you thought you were.

In other words, I felt like the game plan stunk. I believed it had no chance of success.

And yet, as it turned out, we won that game by three touchdowns the next day against a #5-ranked Auburn team. (Having a young Matthew Stafford at quarterback helped a lot with that, of course.) What I'm saying is, you may not always *feel* prepared, even if you worked hard to *be* prepared. Even though I thought our game plan was inadequate, it was actually better than I thought, due to the fact that we'd put the work in.

Preparation always keeps you ahead of where you'd otherwise be. It prevents you from falling prey to that constant state of confusion and uncertainty, where you're most susceptible to making a steady string of foolish choices.

Some people find preparation to be confining. They feel like it cramps their style, that it makes them too rigid, too robotic. But in reality, it sets you free. It's what gives you the momentum, it's what earns you the space, to go off-script when necessary. It's what opens up your life to be able to flex when faced with new opportunities. Since you're grounded where it matters, all your decisions just sort of line up with that.

The point? *Be prepared.*

Always be prepared.

14

Outside the Box

When we first started coaching at Georgia, Katharyn was the only coach's wife allowed to travel on the team plane to away games. Thankfully, most of our opponents' home cities weren't terribly far away, so a lot of the other wives made the trip on their own, but not always.

There was a week, though, when we were playing Ole Miss in Oxford, and for whatever reason, Katharyn was the only one to go—meaning, she didn't have any other coach's wife to sit with. Barbara Dooley, in her typical warm and friendly fashion, invited her to come sit in the AD's box. (The host team usually provides a suite for the visiting school's athletic officials.) But it felt awkward to her. The university president was there, along with other senior staff members. She didn't want to make people uncomfortable having to watch the game alongside the head coach's wife.

Barbara understood, of course, but insisted that Katharyn not spend the game by herself. So at some point they went down on the field and stood together, well beyond the corner of the end zone.

While Katharyn was there watching the game—mainly watching it on the big screen because she could see it so much better than the live-action itself—an idea came to her. What if, instead of ever finding herself in this position again the next year, instead of having to wonder whether any of the other wives were making the trip or not—what if she could find some sort of job to do? Like, what if I'd let her stand behind the bench on the sideline and hand out water to the players? Wouldn't that be fun? Being part of the game day experience like that? Serving the team? (I mean, she was sleeping with the head coach, after all . . . He'd probably be agreeable to it.)

That's how Katharyn became the water girl.

And she loved it. Everybody else loved it too. Including me.

Though unconventional, it actually fell in line with what she'd always enjoyed doing. She had loved being part of my quarterbacks' lives when I was a position coach. When I became a head coach, though, it was hard for her to find a way to be involved. With *all* the players. Problem solved. It was such a hit that she kept it up years later, even when we went to Miami in 2016.

The day she decided not to sit in the box, she made a call that was decidedly outside the box. Some of the best calls we make in life, I've discovered, are often the creative ones, the ones we not only dare to dream up but put into action.

Just ask the water girl.

═══

For our game against Florida in 2007, Katharyn decided to "mix" things up a little. People had taken to calling the Gators' phenomenal sophomore quarterback Tim Tebow "Superman." So she combined the yellow sports drink with the blue sports drink to make green sports drink, and called it *kryptonite*. Whether it helped us beat Florida that year, 42–30, I don't know. But she did help the players be able to picture victory each time they grabbed a cup of their secret weapon.

But there was nothing like the mixture she concocted for our home game against Auburn two weeks later. She stirred in every color available to make something deep purple enough to be almost black. Why black juice? Because it was the perfect match for another "outside the box" idea we had.

The seniors wanted to ask our fans to wear black for that year's Auburn game. I agreed. So our marketing team helped spread the word that the game would be a "Black Out," in the vein of Penn State's "White Out" and other team-color promotions that are popular with fans and players alike. But asking your ticket-paying public to show up at the game in one color of shirts, tops, and caps is one thing. It's just an individual choice. They probably go grab something they already own out of their closet. Getting black jerseys made up for your entire team, however, is not nearly so easy.

That's what I told the seniors when they came over to the house during camp in the fall, before the start of the 2007 season. This informal meeting and lunch was something I did every year—a time for me to just hang out with the graduating class, to pray for their success, and to talk with them about things they hoped to accomplish in the coming season. They asked me that day if we could wear black jerseys for one of our games, same as the previous seniors had asked me the year before.

The first problem with this idea was that Georgia is one of those programs that doesn't like to change the uniform because they have such a classic look. A normal home uni is red jerseys with silver britches. It's already great. Second, I said, "Do you think I can just call Nike up and have a new jersey designed, sewn, and shipped overnight? We would need to ask them, like, a year or more in advance. So forget it. We just can't do it."

Little did they know, it was already in the works.

Still, it was a logistical challenge. Athens, even in the fall, can be hot. No way were we wearing black jerseys for a September game, and all of our October games were unfortunately on the road that year, bookending our bye week on October 20. Home dates in November included games against Troy and

Kentucky—not exactly the right matchups for that sort of rollout. It left only the Auburn week. Okay then. It was all working out. Kickoff was scheduled for the late afternoon, heading toward nightfall. Should be cool and pleasant.

Perfect. Everything was coming together for it.

We were getting untracked after losing a couple of SEC games earlier in the season. Auburn had lost two conference games as well. So we both needed a win badly in order to keep from underperforming by our two schools' lofty standards. We were #10; Auburn was #18.

The black jerseys, though, remained a carefully guarded secret. I knew about it; Katharyn knew about it; our equipment man knew about it. And that was it. I told absolutely no one else. If I remember correctly, I didn't even tell the coaches.

This was going to be fun.

The media, realizing the game had been publicized as a Black Out, asked me about the possibility of us coming out in black jerseys to match. I told them the same thing I'd told the players: "Do you think I can get jerseys that fast?" Of course not. Which was true. Just because we already had them on hand, stowed away where nobody could find them, didn't make what I said a lie, now, did it?

So we came out for the traditional Dawg Walk and warm-ups in our customary red home jerseys. Everything cool. Everything normal. We then jogged off the field and back to our locker room to await the game-time run into the stadium.

One of the team's rituals, at that part of the pregame—dating back before my time at Georgia—was to turn off all the lights in the dressing room and gather in the shower area. Just the players by themselves. One of them would give a fiery speech of some kind, followed by someone else saying a quick prayer. It lasted only a few minutes. But it happened every week.

This was my window.

I'd told the equipment guy, John Meshad, "The second the lights go out—I don't care how many people it takes you to do it—make sure those black jerseys are folded in the players' lockers when they come back in." I, meanwhile, was off in the coach's locker room, changing into my own black outfit: black shoes, black shirt, black pants, the whole works. Johnny Cash would have been proud.

Through the wall I could hear the players breaking up from their team huddle. I could see the lights snap back on, gleaming under the doorway.

All I heard then was delirium. They went nuts. By the time I came out from where I'd been dressing, the locker room was so hot that it was steaming. Literal steam.

There stood the players in their new black jerseys, sweating and breathing hard, practically pawing the ground to get out on the field. I was almost afraid I'd overplayed the secrecy element. They looked nearly exhausted already, simply from the joy of their reaction. I wondered if they'd have any energy left for the game. But they flew through the tunnel and sprinted out onto the field, leaping and fist-pumping and high-stepping. Uncontainable emotion. Our unsuspecting fans went completely berserk.

Best of all, we won the game. (Nothing like getting everybody worked up and then losing. Ask me how I know: "Black Out: The 2008 Version" against Alabama.) But every Georgia fan remembers the first one—the real one—the night we broke the black jerseys out of the box.

———

This was also the year—2007—that I began doing my annual backflip off the high dive during fall camp.

Throughout the monotony of two-a-day practices—which were still common at that time, before the NCAA put limits on them in 2017—we as coaches were already smart enough to know we needed to watch our team, to recognize when the heat and fatigue were becoming too much, putting them in danger of injury, or worse. So one day, during our normal team meeting before practice, I said to the players, with a perfectly straight face, "Men, we've got a tough decision to make." It was already sweltering hot, of course, even in the morning, Georgia in August. "We're going to do one of two things to start our day today: we're either going out to practice, or we're going to the Ramsey," the Ramsey Student Center—which they knew to mean, the swimming pool.

The two seconds of stunned silence and sideways glances that hung there in the meeting room in that moment were priceless. After that, roaring cheers. They jumped out of their seats; they ran to the buses. We'd turned some tired Dawgs into one happy bunch.

From then on, it became a tradition. Every year—and they never knew exactly when—*one* of these days of fall practice, they knew, we were going to the Ramsey.

One time, for instance, we had a scrimmage scheduled at the stadium rather than on the practice fields that day. After everybody got taped, got dressed, did their various group meetings, and crowded onto the buses, we began our caravan to that part of campus. (The stadium is a good distance away from where we practiced; you wouldn't just walk it.) But as we drew near, the buses continued going, slowing down, but then looping on around the stadium, heading south. "Where are we going?" You could feel the confusion rippling through the conversations on the bus.

Then recognition.

We're going to the Ramsey!

I hadn't even told the other coaches about it, same as during the Black Out. In fact, our special teams coach, who was so meticulous in preparation, had already gone early to the stadium to set up what we wanted to work on that day. His labor wouldn't be wasted, of course; we would still do the same scrimmage as planned. We'd just do it later. First, today, we were going swimming.

And part of each year's swim, the players knew, was my back flip off the ten-meter board—the tallest platform, the one that's way up there.

I'm not sure what everybody saw in it. At first I think it was just to prove to everybody that, yeah, the old man could really do it. But soon it grew into more of a motivational thing. The team expected it. Especially as the years went by, first at Georgia and then at Miami, as my body looked less and less like the Boca Baby persona of my younger days, the sight of the head coach fearlessly falling backward and releasing from three stories high—it does something to knit a little camaraderie between yourself and your players.

I guess the real genesis of it goes back to being a south Florida teenager. We used to jump from the Boca Raton Inlet Bridge to show off to the girls. It was a little over a twenty-foot drop, so even a pencil jump carried at least a modicum of danger and daring. But one of the surfer dudes, a kid named Kenny, could do a backflip off that bridge, which was extraordinarily cooler. I finally just had to humble myself and say, "Man, you've gotta teach me how to do that." And once you get over the horror of it, especially if you're adolescent enough not to be worried about breaking your neck, you get the hang of it. The technique sort of never changes. It sticks with you.

It's pretty exhilarating, really, even now, being thirty-something feet high, turning and falling into the arms of gravity. In some ways, I think it's a stereotype-shattering picture of what God wants our life of faith to look like. Faith and following Christ is not a dull, hold-your-nose jump off the springboard. It's not resigning yourself to things that are small and confining. *Sin* is what's confining. Sin is what tightens around us until we're trapped and imbedded into our addictions. It doesn't make us *more;* it makes us *less.*

In Jesus, life opens up.

For instance, each fall at the University of Georgia, right at the beginning of the semester, they always held a campus-wide pep rally. It was the unofficial kickoff to the school year, scheduled for the Friday before our first home game. As coach, I was usually asked to be one of the speakers, and every year I would use it as an opportunity to say a prayer over the student body—the ones who'd chosen to come that day—asking God to keep them safe, to watch over them, to help them care for one another. Everybody seemed to appreciate that.

Faith and following Christ is not a dull, hold-your-nose jump off the springboard. It's not resigning yourself to things that are small and confining.

There came a year, however, when it looked like I wouldn't be able to do that anymore. One of those activist groups that gets bent out of shape whenever anything slightly religious happens on campus took objection to my public praying—noisy enough that the school administration heard of it, got queasy about it, and decided the blowback wasn't worth it. Without telling me what to do or not do, they kindly got the point across that it might be better all the way around if I just didn't end my speech with a prayer anymore.

Well.

Let's see if I really had to live inside that box.

I talked with a constitutional lawyer who knew the legal dos and don'ts of this type of thing. He said, yeah, if you were dealing with high school kids at a mandatory event, you might have yourself a problem. But if your audience is made up of people who are eighteen years of age or older (which it was) and who aren't required to be there (which they weren't), you are well within your legal rights to do all the praying you want, to whomever you want to pray.

So I could technically do it, but I also knew how our administration felt about it. What should I do?

The answer came to me the night before. As I was praying to God, He gave me an idea.

I went to the big event the next day. Hundreds of people in attendance. My turn came to speak, then I reached the part where I would customarily offer my prayer. I said to the group, "Last night before I went to bed, I was thinking about you guys. And I prayed for you. And this is what I prayed for . . ."

I then told them, not in the form of a prayer but more in the form of a report, exactly what I'd spoken with the Lord about. I mentioned all the things I would ordinarily have addressed directly to Him in their presence. I just didn't say it in a way that could get anybody in trouble for it.

Thank You, God!

Because believers, see, we don't live in a box. Believers get to live in wide, open spaces where everything is possible because our God is truly unlimited.

15

Turnovers

I love calling plays. It's a lot of fun.

Some of my favorite times in football were as an offensive coordinator at Florida State, sitting up in the booth on game day with the whole field laid out before me. It was almost like a video game. I'm more of a visual guy, I guess, a visual learner. (I think most men are that way.) And the chess match of being able to take in the whole game board from a bird's-eye perspective, and then move your pieces around in anticipation of what your opponent is thinking . . .

Man, it's exhilarating. Few things in football gave me quite the thrill as that moment when—when it clicked. The instant you knew *exactly* which play to run. And when it worked.

I knew our system so well; I knew what I liked to do. More important, I knew what our players could do. So I thrived on that moment when the play call was in, watching the defense set up. You already knew where the ball was going because you'd trained your quarterback so well that you trusted he would make the right decision. Once he makes that decision, of course, he still needs to have protection; he still needs to throw an accurate pass; the receiver still has to catch it. Everybody has a job to do. But when they all do it right, it's a thing of beauty. It's like its own little symphony of preparation and instinct, of practice and players, intertwining into a living diagram of X's and O's.

And as an offensive coordinator, you can afford to just lose yourself in that. All through the offseason, all I did was study football, study offenses, study defenses, preparing myself to be ready once I was back in the booth in the fall.

Then I became a head coach. And the head coach can't spend his whole offseason studying football, studying offenses, studying defenses. He's shaking hands. He's meeting boosters. He's giving interviews. He's raising money. He's on the radio. He's on the speaking circuit. He's on the caravan to neighboring towns and gatherings to sign autographs and smile for selfies.

I'm not complaining. And to tell you the truth, I genuinely enjoyed that stuff for the most part because of the people I got to meet in the process. I really did.

It's just that football coaches, down in their gut, love *football*. That's what first draws them in. They want to stay around football. It's almost like wanting to keep being a kid, just forever playing and thinking about football.

And so while I felt blessed beyond words to be head coach at the University of Georgia, I couldn't imagine it getting in the way of what I considered my greatest strengths as a football coach: running the offense, coaching quarterbacks, and calling plays.

Coach Bowden had done it, wearing both hats. He was a terrific play caller. One of the best ever. But no doubt, it takes a lot of extra time, staying in charge of that aspect. It naturally adds a big extra piece to what occupies your mind during a ball game. Not only that, but being on the sideline as a head coach limits what you can see. Many times in reviewing game film, I would think to myself, "Shoot, if I was in the booth, I would've called a different play there." From the sidelines you see details; you see pieces of things. And in some ways, by being so close to what's happening, you gain certain advantages in your play calling that the booth doesn't provide. But you miss seeing the big picture. You're restricted to getting only audio descriptions in your ear of what your staff is seeing and telling you from topside. And I'm a visual learner, remember? Not audio.

Still, you can make it work, like Coach Bowden made it work. But it's taxing over time, something he recognized, too, after a while. Following the 1991 season at Florida State, where we lost our #1 ranking late in the year, dropping two games in the last two weeks to Miami ("Wide Right I") and Florida, then barely beating Texas A&M in the Cotton Bowl by the odd score of 10–2, he sensed it was time to delegate those responsibilities. He came to the offensive staff during the offseason and said he'd decided to turn the play calling over to us.

I wasn't yet the offensive coordinator. I was the quarterbacks coach and, as you may recall, was considered the unofficial passing game coordinator. But between Brad Scott and myself, we began calling the plays from that point forward, beginning in 1992, Charlie Ward's first year as the starter.

So, I'd seen it work. I'd seen what new, fresh eyes had to offer.

But there's a difference in perspective between being the young, ambitious assistant who's being entrusted with greater responsibility and the older, more seasoned coach entrusting your offense to someone younger on your staff. And yet there comes a time for each of us, in whatever kind of work we do, to turn some things over . . . so that we can be our best and so that others can grow.

━━━

Jesus modeled this approach. Even though, gosh, if anybody ever needed *no* assistants to turn *anything* over to, it would be Jesus. He called the right plays at every moment of every day. But He was building a team. He was teaching a new system. He was giving them (and us) a guide for how leaders multiply themselves in those real-life situations where none of us is, you know, God. No matter how good we may be at a certain skill, or at *many* skills, we humans possess limitations that we ignore at our own peril.

Turnovers are bad in football; turnovers are essential in life.

And so I knew the day would come. Wasn't sure when. But when it did, it had to be the right person. The only call that's as important as knowing when to pass the baton is knowing what you're looking for in the person you're passing it off to.

Turnovers are bad in football; turnovers are essential in life. And, again, the reason I knew to be grooming someone for that task was because I'd been taught it by a wise mentor before he eventually turned it over himself.

My first year at Georgia, having hired Neil Callaway as offensive coordinator, I also hired Mike Bobo as quarterbacks coach, someone who could work with me the same way I'd worked with Coach Bowden at Florida State. I couldn't focus as much time individually on the QBs as they needed, being both the head coach *and* play caller. But I could show Mike how I wanted it done. I could teach him the terminology I wanted to use with the quarterbacks so that we would always be communicating the same things, always speaking the same language, whether it was coming from Mike or from me. Always being on the same page.

Mike, you may know, was a prolific Bulldog quarterback in the mid- to late-'90s, and he'd already worked a stint as a graduate assistant under Jim Donnan shortly after his playing days. When I hired him as a full-time assistant, he showed up day-one with a sharp coach's mind, and over time I watched him grow into the role. At the beginning, I would take the lead myself in installing the plays with the quarterbacks while Mike watched and asked questions, offering good suggestions. But after a few years, he was the one leading the room while I sat on and watched. We developed a level of rapport where we trusted one another, understood one another, and—as borne out, I think, by the overall success of our offense—were good for one another.

But I reached that point where, like Coach Bowden did, I felt like my effectiveness as a play caller, combined with all the other duties and obligations of being a head coach, had dipped a bit. So as we got ready for our bowl against Virginia Tech at the end of the 2006 season, I told him I wanted him to call the plays for that game. I said, "Mike, if we win, I'll tell everybody you called the game. If we lose, we won't say anything. They'll just assume I was still calling the plays." I didn't think it was fair to announce someone publicly in that position without giving him a full offseason to prepare and put things together exactly the way he wanted. But I knew he could do it. And he did a great job, not only in our victory that day, but in many other victories throughout his long stay as offensive coordinator, after Neil left to become head coach at Alabama-Birmingham (UAB).

The right time. The right person. The right reasons for making the call.

But then—and this is equally important—you've got to give that person the space to learn and struggle and find their own level, to try things that might differ sometimes from the way you would've done them. He won't be able to focus if you're in his ear the whole time.

What I'm about to say, I say with no disrespect for Coach Bowden because I have zero disrespect for Coach Bowden. *Minus-zero*, if that's possible. The only reason I say it is because I think it's funny, and I think you'll find it funny too.

In my first game of calling plays at Florida State, we came to our first third-down situation, and if memory serves, I called Red 200 Exxon—the same pass play that I mentioned to you before, how I blurted it out during the Kansas game my first year on the job. It went for a winning touchdown that day, as you recall, mainly because Kansas came out in zero coverage.

In *this* game, however, after I called Red 200 Exxon, the defense lined up in Cover 2, which meant the square-in would be the quarterback's first progression instead of the deep post. Charlie, who was playing his first game as the starter, sailed it over the receiver's head as he was cutting across the middle. The ball got picked. Bad turnover. I hear Coach Bowden say in my headset, "Dadgum it, I wouldn't have called that play." So that was my vote of confidence, right out of the chute.

In another game I remember, not long after that, I called a reverse. A trick play, right? I don't recall exactly how it did. It wasn't an epic fail, I don't think—it could've been worse—but still, it didn't amount to much, just a hyperactive couple of yards. Coach: "Dadgum it, I'm the only one who calls trick plays around here."

Again, just funny, I think.

When we'd be going through times where the offense wasn't looking quite as crisp, when we weren't scoring every time we got the ball, Coach might say to me, offhand, "Have you got it, buddy? Do you need any help?" Every so often I'd get my feelings hurt at that. I'd go into his office on the Sunday afternoon or Monday after the game and say, "Coach, you know, if you'd like to go back to calling plays, I've got no problem with that." I meant it sincerely.

"No, buddy," he'd say, "don't listen to me. You're doing a good job. I'll try to catch you in between series from now on."

Of course he had the right to say whatever he wanted, whenever he wanted. I just appreciated him wanting to allow me to stay focused in the heat of the game. He and I had just a terrific relationship.

So when it came my turn to be in his shoes at Georgia, I tried to stay out of Mike's way, too, because I understood the dynamic from both ends. If I had a suggestion, I made it between series or at some other logical break in the action.

It can be a bit of a dance, these turnovers we need to make in our lives. A little awkward and uncomfortable sometimes. But they're worth it. They're worth the effort. They're worth the humility and the willingness to change.

They're a win-win situation.

━━━

So did I make the wrong call? From the start? By ever choosing to be my own play caller at Georgia? I don't think so. It helped me put a deeper stamp on the offense. It helped me grow in areas where I already excelled while also being able to learn more readily, more rapidly, the things that worked in this new environment.

As well as the things that didn't.

Take, for example, our first year, 2001—another Auburn game that sticks in my mind. We were at home. Close game, trailing by a touchdown, but driving with under a minute to go. David Greene threw a long completion to Terrence Edwards that put us on the 1-yard line. We were right at the doorstep of scoring. Sixteen seconds to go. No time-outs.

Make the call.

First, let's talk a little ball: turn of the century, SEC-style. Few people, from the referees on the field to the coaches on the other sideline, were excited about adjusting to the hurry-up style of offense that I was bringing into the conference from Florida State. The personnel groupings were a little different from what we'd run there, because I'd inherited two future NFL tight ends at Georgia in Randy McMichael and Ben Watson, but the formations and philosophy were the same. Again, this was prior to rule changes that required giving the defense ample time to substitute personnel. In that era, offenses could make whatever adjustments they wanted, no matter how late in the play clock, and the defense just had to stand pat with the players they had on the field and do the best they could. I'm not saying this was a *good* rule, just that it *was* the rule in 2001, so there was nothing wrong with using it to your competitive advantage. If the pace of play moved too fast for your opponent to properly set up their defense—if it didn't even give enough time for the referees themselves to hustle into position and be ready for the ball to be snapped—that wasn't my problem. Unless they decided to *make* it my problem.

So, given my understanding of the rules, my plan following a long pass to the 1 was to sprint in our big guys, moving at a fast pace, replacing the three-receiver set that had just been on the field, faster than the defense could adjust. We would then set up in an unbalanced look (like, say, with two tackles on one side of the ball), create a little chaos, making it hard for the defensive linemen to quickly figure out where to line up. Then we'd snap the ball on first sound and basically just walk in. The other team might even make it easier on us by getting flagged for having thirteen men on the field, while trying to hustle players in from the sideline to the goal line. That's a long run, both ways, for big guys.

But this wasn't the ACC anymore, Mark. And while the rulebook said I could do it, I believe the refs had their own plans for slowing this mess down. So, even like right here, where they should've just marked the ball on the 1 and let us snap the ball quickly, instead they stepped in, held up play, waited for the defense to get all sweet lined up, and—with no time-outs for us to work with—we had to stay committed to our play call. The Auburn defense plugged the hole, stuffed the run, took forever unpiling from the ball carrier, and we never got another snap off.

Coach looked dumb. Because, obviously, with sixteen seconds, we could've thrown a pass in that situation, probably *two* passes. *Then* try to run if we wanted. So truthfully, maybe I *was* dumb.

But I was learning. Learning to be the head coach as well as the play caller. Learning to improve in my clock management. (Remember, we hadn't played in too many close games at Florida State; the clock didn't usually figure into the outcome too often.) I was also learning to deal with the media, where I simply owned the mistake that I'd made and acknowledged I'd robbed us of a couple of chances to score, a couple of extra chances to tie and hopefully win the game.

These learning opportunities—when I responded to them humbly—earned me some loyalty points with our players and staff, and together we did some pretty good things as a ball team. We won more than sixty games in those first six years. Won the SEC twice. Won the East three times. Something like a 78 percent winning percentage overall.

Still, even with that kind of success, it didn't mean the time wouldn't come when a new organizational chart would be the best option for carrying our success forward. You've got to be ready to recognize that. To make that call. To create turnovers that help your team keep winning.

16

The ~~Dog~~ Dawg Pile

We didn't play Alabama every year. But let the record show, we won our first three games against them. The first was in 2002, on the road at Tuscaloosa, fondly remembered by Georgia fans as the "Man Enough" game. Former Auburn coach Pat Dye had said on sports radio in Birmingham during the week that the Bulldogs weren't "man enough" to take down Alabama at home. Turns out, we weren't only man enough to do it but were able to come back and win after squandering a twelve-point lead. Final score: 27–25.

In 2003, we took them down again, in Athens. But in 2007, Nick Saban was in the house and he was beginning to right the ship. In a hurry. The Tide was 3–0 and ranked in the top twenty—higher than us—when we trucked into Tuscaloosa for an SEC East versus West nighttime showdown that was high on the college football visibility calendar.

We pulled ahead early, staking a 10–0 second-quarter lead. They caught us in the third. But then we put together a long scoring drive, capped by a Knowshon Moreno touchdown run on a toss around right end. After we'd stretched the lead to ten again on a fourth-quarter field goal, quarterback John Parker Wilson led the Bama offense back, tying the game at 20 with just over a minute to play. We were able to work the clock and maneuver into field goal range with a chance to win it in regulation, but the forty-two-yard attempt hooked a few feet left. Headed to overtime.

Bama got the ball first. Our defense stiffened, holding them to a field goal. The score stood at 23–20 as we lined up first and ten at the 25 in a two-receiver set. The tight end backed off the line and went into motion left, staying in to block as Matthew Stafford looked that direction and launched a deep ball toward little 160-pound Mikey Henderson, streaking one-on-one to the goal line. Caught. Touchdown. Ball game.

And then . . .

The winning end zone began filling up with Georgia players, leaping onto each other in one of my favorite images in all of sports: the "Dog Pile."

Check that: the *Dawg* Pile.

━━━━

What do you love most about football, Coach? I love the Dog Pile. The wild celebration after a great victory. I've been fortunate enough to witness several of them over the years, like in this 2007 game at Bryant-Denney, or after our 2001 "Finish the Drill" win against Tennessee, the "Hobnail Boot." The only thing to me, in college football, that runs a close second to the fun and exuberance of the Dog Pile is when you announce to your team that you're awarding a scholarship to one of their walk-on teammates. Everybody jumps out of their seats and shouts and cheers, coming down to get around the guy, clapping him on the back, going crazy together. That's pretty awesome too.

From a distance, I guess, my fascination with the Dog Pile goes back (like yours, probably) to the television images of the final pitch, the final strike, the final out of each year's World Series in baseball. I remember loving to watch that as a kid—all the players streaming toward the pitcher's mound, piling into a heap to celebrate the end of a championship season.

On a personal level, however, my affection for it goes back to a far less pleasurable moment, and yet a night when the Dog Pile took on a much deeper resonance for me.

Florida State in 1995 was enjoying another highlight-reel season. We'd hit seventy points three times already that year, not against patsies, but against conference opponents. When we weren't scoring in the seventies, we were at minimum scoring in the forties. Seven games, seven big wins. And yet even more phenomenal than the success of that single season was the string of victories we'd put together since joining the ACC in 1992. Twenty-nine in a row. We were going on four years now of an unblemished conference record.

It had gotten to where, to be honest with you, we didn't do a lot of celebrating after (another) win. Winning had become sort of old hat. Maybe if we'd just gotten through beating Florida or Miami, or maybe if it was a bowl game—maybe *then* the locker room would feel electric with players celebrating. But for the most part, winning was just another day at the office. It's honestly hard to keep that from happening. Most coaches would love having that problem.

But this was the mood we took into Charlottesville for a Thursday night ESPN game against Virginia. They were probably the best team we'd played to that point in the year. George Welsh had built UVA into a consistently strong program for the first time in, I think, forever. They were now in the habit of going to a bowl game every year. They were not an easy out. This particular year's team was 6–3 by the time of our game on November 2, but two of those losses had been one-point affairs on the road against #14 Michigan and #16 Texas. Tiki and Ronde Barber were both on that team—probably the best-known names today—along with senior quarterback Mike Groh, whose father, Al Groh, would later succeed Welsh as Virginia's head coach. But those guys were not alone. The '95 Cavaliers had good players on both sides of the ball.

And believing fans.

Capacity at Scott Stadium in those years was a little north of 44,000. It wasn't a big place. The seating on one end was like a grassy hillside, where people could sit in families on the lawn. On any other night, their kids could probably run around and play, too, but it was loud and packed and energetic on *this* night. Great atmosphere for football.

We were winning at first, until we weren't—until they blocked a punt early in the second quarter and converted it into a field goal to take their first lead of the game. Then they stayed out ahead of us—big enough and long enough to get the faithful in the stands thinking they might actually be in store for a miracle.

And yet, we found a way. Like always. Despite seeming to dig our own grave near the end there, by throwing an interception at around the two-and-a-half-minute mark, we got the ball back. And after cranking up our offense, we found ourselves at the 6-yard line with nine seconds left—trailing by five, 33–28, but with the winning end zone a very makeable distance away. It all came down to this final series.

Fans and students, just in case, were already bunched up at the base of that berm area, directly under the opposite goal post. Our first-down play was an incompletion, stopping the clock at four seconds. And yet a large number of people, seeing that pass fall to the ground, rushed the field prematurely, some of them advancing as far as the 50-yard line. Virginia players and coaches frantically yelled and waved their arms, fearing a penalty, telling everybody to get back, that the game wasn't over.

On the next play—sure to be the last play—we centered the ball to running back Warrick Dunn on a direct snap. Trickery.

Not many teams in college football ran the wildcat then. I thought it was a good call because on the play prior they'd been in a prevent defense, meaning they were anticipating a pass. I actually thought we'd scored on it. Even the TV announcer initially called a touchdown. But Warrick had gotten tripped at around the 3, then stumbled forward, falling, stretching, ultimately landing with his head and shoulders right on the goal line, but with the ball inches from going across. Or was it? Instant replay might have said touchdown.

Didn't matter. We'd lost.

The place came apart.

Amid the bedlam, I'm up there in the booth, packing my stuff, getting ready to leave. Instead of having an elevator to carry you down to the locker room area, your only option was to walk directly through the stands, like everybody else—which, under normal conditions meant weaving into the flow of foot traffic with other people exiting the stadium. But on this night, the stands had pretty much emptied out. Most everybody had exited onto the playing field. So it only took me a few minutes to make my lonely descent to the ground to go meet up with the team.

Well, again, the unusual design and dynamics of Scott Stadium. When you reached the bottom of the stairs, you hung a left to go to the locker room. But on the way to the *visitor's* locker room, you first had to pass the *Virginia* locker room.

The door was standing wide open, and inside was one of the most unhinged, irrepressible, indescribable Dog Piles of a moment that I'd ever witnessed. I didn't slow down to watch much, of course, but I definitely took notice. And I thought to myself, "I wonder what that feels like."

Actually, I never forgot that feeling.

It's why one of the things I deliberately tried to do when I got to Georgia was not rush too quickly past the victories, even the more expected victories. We needed to take time to celebrate. We worked so hard, we poured so much of ourselves into those wins. *All* of us did. And I didn't want our team to just flip the switch toward the next game and next opponent without celebrating our victory in *this* week's game, over *this* opponent, on *this* day.

Stop and celebrate.

It's important. It's important in football; it's important in life.

"Stop and smell the roses" is, I think, too cliché of a way to put it anymore. We don't even hear when people say that. Knowing we should do it doesn't keep us from continuing to move too fast. Rarely do we take the time to absorb what's good and of immediate importance right around us, the blessings we can't seem to fully enjoy because our minds are already thinking ahead, wanting something else.

So I kind of like how author G. K. Chesterton said it, a British writer of the twentieth century. He talked of how we become "weary of wonders"—like, how if we were to see the sun for the first time, we would think it's the most incredible thing ever. But because we see it every day, because we've seen it hundreds and thousands of times, we don't even look out the window for it in the morning. We don't think anything about it. The sun's up again? Big deal. And yet if we persist in approaching life that way, we'll miss something extremely valuable in the process.

Rarely do we take the time to absorb what's good and of immediate importance right around us, the blessings we can't seem to fully enjoy because our minds are already thinking ahead, wanting something else.

I changed up my pregame habits a little, not too long after that Virginia spectacle. Even if only for a couple of moments, whether as offensive coordinator at Florida State or as head coach at Georgia and Miami, I would try to stop after coming out onto the field, despite my mind being focused on the upcoming game, and just lift my head and take in the atmosphere. Relish the sights and sounds of a college football stadium on game day. *Look where you are, Mark. This is nuts. This is awesome. Not everybody gets to do this.*

Stop and celebrate.

And I challenge you to do the same. There's too much to thank God for, right here, right now. There are too many ordinary places that hide life's deepest beauties in plain sight, if we'd only be looking for them. There are too many people who help us achieve whatever we achieve in life for us to run past a moment of any significance without stopping to include them in it, to express our appreciation for their hand in it.

We really should be part of more Dog Piles.

All right, so let's talk about the Dog Pile of all *Dawg* Piles— the infamous unsportsmanlike, bench-clearing, first-quarter celebration penalty at the Florida game in 2007. I don't suppose it carries the weight of one of those cultural events where you "remember where you were" when it took place or when you first saw it or heard about it. But I sure do remember where I was. And no matter what anybody says or thinks, I was actually, at that moment, just about as dumbfounded by it as anybody.

Here's the real story.

Like I said, that FSU loss at Virginia never really left me. More than once in my time as offensive coordinator for the Seminoles in the years following that game, whenever I would spot a lack of energy or excitement in our players—whenever we'd win another game by a big mash-up of points and everybody would shower and change like they'd just gotten off work—I would jump on my offensive guys the next week in practice. I'd tell them I needed to see some more life. I might even say something crazy, like, "In this next game, the first time we score, I want y'all to celebrate on the field until we get a flag, all right?"

"On the field" was the operative phrase. I was talking about the players *on* the field *when* we scored. "You let me deal with Coach Bowden if he gets mad about it, but we need some juice, men. I want to see some excessive celebration."

So I'd walked this line of thinking in times past. It wasn't unlike me. It's just that it had been a while since I'd felt that way about our Georgia team.

But I quickly got to that point after the Vanderbilt game.

Seems like every time we went to Vanderbilt, we barely eked out a victory. Bobby Johnson–coached teams through that stretch of the 2000s were beginning to improve, but still, we should never have had the trouble handling them that we often did. They actually beat us in Athens the year before on a last-second field goal, and the 2007 game in Nashville was tight again. They led 17–7 at the half. It took a last-second field goal of our own to emerge with a three-point win.

I don't know if it was the crowd or the atmosphere or what. Unlike most SEC campuses on a Saturday afternoon, Vanderbilt football is not the only game in town, not in Music City. The stadium is fairly small, and the attendance at games against high-profile conference opponents is typically skewed in favor of the visitors. It's just a little weird that way. But, not making excuses. We just came out flat and stayed flat. And nearly lost. And I wasn't happy. I knew if we stayed at anywhere near this level of disinterest and dispassion, we were going to get killed in two weeks against Florida.

Fortunately, by the wisdom of the schedule makers, our next week was an open date. So I stood in front of our team, before those two weeks of practice, and threw down the same appeal that I'd made to the Seminole offense in a similar situation, hoping it would spark something inside them I hadn't seen at

Vandy but *needed* to see at Jacksonville. "Listen, when we play Florida? The first score? We're gonna celebrate on the field till they throw a flag on us."

On the field.

The eleven players *on the field.*

That's again what I saw in my mind when I gave the order.

During practice in those two weeks, I was already seeing the players more animated. The offense would score a touchdown against the scout team, and the guy who scored would spin the ball or spike it over the goalpost or something. Okay. But all I saw were people doing individual things like that. "Look-at-me" kind of stuff. They weren't doing it as a team thing. And that bothered me. I didn't say anything about it, but it was in my craw a little bit as we got ready to head to Jacksonville.

When we were meeting in the hotel the night before the game, I brought my concerns to the team. "I've been telling you guys, after our first touchdown, we're going to celebrate enough to get a penalty, right?" *Right.* "And if you *don't* celebrate enough to get a penalty, I'm gonna run your butts in practice next week, all right?" *All right.*

"Well, I've been watching you guys in practice, doing all this individual crap, and I want you to know, that's not what I'm talking about. I want it to be a team celebration"—again, thinking "team celebration" included the players who'd be on the field at that instant, the unit who'd done the actual, physical blocking and running to score that first touchdown.

"Which, by the way," I wanted to be sure to clarify, "if we don't score in the first quarter, this thing is off. If we're getting beat 40–0 and we score a pointless touchdown in the fourth quarter, I don't want any penalty called against us for that, all right?"

I wanted a celebration . . .

Early in the game . . .

On the field . . .

When we score . . .

Enough to draw a flag.

I thought I'd made myself clear enough.

Obviously not.

Florida got the opening kick, drove it into our territory, fumbled the ball. We recovered and ran it back past midfield, where we started our first possession around the 40. On the ninth play of the drive—all running plays—Knowshon took a third-and-goal handoff over the top from inside the 2, stretching the nose of the football barely over the goal line.

Touchdown.

And there they went. Everybody.

The entire football team ran out and celebrated in the end zone.

Now by the time I realized what was happening—by the time the cameras swung over to see my reaction—I was resigned to what the guys had done. Cat was out of the bag by then. Nothing I could really do except go along with it. In fact, as soon as it happened, there was this one player who'd stayed standing over there beside me after the whole rest of the bench had swarmed the field. I looked at him, sort of puzzled. He said, "Coach, you know I've been in the doghouse. I'm not going out there and getting myself in any more trouble." But, long story short, if the camera had caught me while the bodies were streaming past me, they'd have seen me with an expression of disbelief on my face, like, "What in the world . . ."

This was *not* what I meant everybody to do. Not *everybody.*

But then it got even more interesting. If I somehow looked like a motivational genius for orchestrating a flagrant rule violation to rile up our players and fans, I was about to look like a complete idiot for maybe costing us a touchdown. I mean, this was a rivalry game that I had lost five times out of six. We could not afford to be taking points off the board.

The touchdown call on the field went to instant replay for review, to see if the ball crossed the goal line. If it hadn't, the score would be 0–0 again. And instead of having the ball on the one-inch line, we'd be backed up third and goal from just beyond the 15. Actually, worse—because we'd also drawn a *second* unsportsmanlike flag, charged to an individual player for excessive celebration. That was another fifteen yards. It'd be third and goal from the 30. And Coach might be looking for a new job.

To my sheer relief, the touchdown was upheld. My "genius" remained intact. And though we temporarily lost the field-position battle by having to kick off from our seven-and-a-half, we wound up winning the ball game in fairly convincing fashion. Katharyn's *kryptonite* game. It jump-started us to an unbeaten, season-ending run, culminating in a solid defeat of Georgia Tech to close out the regular schedule, and a 41–10 romp over Hawaii (who was surprisingly good that year) to win the Sugar Bowl and finish in the top five.

So don't give me too much credit for being the mad-scientist sports psychologist who went to the right bag of tricks to fire up his football team. I got the party started, yes, but my only other contribution was just to play along with it when it got out of hand. It might have looked more like a *pack* of 'Dogs than a *pile* of 'Dogs, but it was something worth celebrating.

And that's the truth.

=====

The next year, in the week leading up to the Florida game, all the talk was about our shenanigans from the year before. Both teams were tied atop the SEC East standings. Our only loss since being there last November was a 41–30 defeat at the hands of undefeated Alabama, who was currently the #1 team in the nation. The joint was jumping.

All you need to know, if you can't instantly recall the 2008 game, is that we scored late to pull within forty. Let that number settle with you for a second. We'd been taken to the woodshed. And you'd think to Coach Urban Meyer, a 49–10 dismantling of your main obstacle to the conference championship game (eventually the *national* championship game, which they would go on to win against #2 Oklahoma) would be sufficient salt in the wound to avenge last season's embarrassment.

No.

With forty-four seconds left, the game mercifully reached its kneel-down point. Victory formation, right? Final play for the win? Not so fast. Urban called a time-out while Tim Tebow and his teammates roamed the sidelines, their backs turned to the field, whipping the crowd into a frenzy of victorious euphoria—after which, still operating out of the shotgun, they ripped off a fifteen-yard run around left end for a first down. *Now* they'd kneel, surely.

No.

Another time-out with thirty seconds left. Another towel-waving, sideline love fest between players and Gator fans, extending for the full time allotted by another block of television commercials.

Again operating from the shotgun, they took it around left end for *another* first down, before he finally decided he'd gotten his pound of flesh.

And while I'm not saying I appreciated it, I have to say I thought it was a pretty good response on his part, to be honest with you. They got their payback. "He who laughs last" and all that.

Take a moment to stop and celebrate, is what I always say. I guess even a Gator can do it sometimes too.

I know one thing: you'll be glad *you* did it.

17

The Fine Line

September in SEC football is a time for hopefully banking a couple of victories against mid-major or in-state opponents. It presumably gets your team off to a winning start and gives your backups a chance to get some live action in order to help build your depth.

September 2013, however, was not one of those months at Georgia.

We started out on a Saturday night at Dabo Swinney's #8 Clemson, followed by our home opener the next week against Steve Spurrier's #6 South Carolina. Then, as if September hadn't had enough big games already, Les Miles brought his 4-0 LSU Tigers into town on the final weekend of the month, having climbed the polls to a #6 ranking themselves, led by a well-traveled senior quarterback . . . someone we knew a thing or two about.

Zach Mettenberger not only signed to play with us at Georgia in 2009 but had grown up ten minutes south of Athens, dreaming of being a Bulldog ever since coming to his first game at Sanford Stadium as a seven-year-old. In the same recruiting class with Zach was another blue-chip prospect, a young player from Tampa named Aaron Murray, setting up what was sure to be a stiff competition between two freshman quarterbacks coming into camp.

As a result of injury and other circumstances, both Zach and Aaron red-shirted their 2009 season. But the following year, 2010, soon after spring practice, Zach was dismissed from the team after not behaving the way he should. He subsequently played a season of community college ball in Kansas before transferring to LSU in 2011. Add a turn of events here and there, and by September 28, 2013, he was set to go up against his former teammates at Georgia, on his former playing field at Georgia, against his former roommate at Georgia, our four-year starting quarterback, Aaron Murray.

"Aaron versus Zach" was the featured storyline heading into the game, personalized even further by the fact that Zach's mom, Tammy, worked in our athletic office. I'd given her the week off so that she could choose for herself how many people she wanted to be around and how many questions she wanted to answer. She deserved to be just a mom watching her son play football, I thought.

And what a game it was. Both quarterbacks were incredible. Impressive performances all around. Even with tailback Todd Gurley going down with an ankle sprain in the first half, even though we were going up against a potent LSU offense that included guys like Jarvis Landry and Odell Beckham Jr. at wide receiver, we were able to throw the last punch in a colossal, back-and-forth clash between two great college football programs.

There was never more than a touchdown's difference in the score the whole ball game. Zach led a drive midway through the fourth that put LSU four points ahead, but Aaron and our two-minute offense answered. His twenty-five-yard touchdown pass with under two minutes to go proved to be the deciding margin.

We'd been part of another SEC slugfest. We'd put it all out there on the field on a Saturday afternoon in September, and we had won, 44–41.

Sometimes the difference between winning and losing is like that—a matter of feet and inches, of minutes and seconds. We won the game that day. A tremendous win. But what if we'd lost? It wouldn't have been from a lack of effort or preparation, I can tell you that. It wouldn't have been a matter of overlooking an opponent or downplaying what was at stake. We did our best. We did enough to win. Obviously. But what if when the dust had cleared that day, what if when everything was settled, what if we'd come up a little short? Would that have made us a loser?

In football, you understand that's the way it is. The line is that thin. If you try something that works, you're brilliant. If you try something that doesn't work, you're a bum. Okay. That's fine. That's what we coaches signed up for. But you get good at telling yourself that even if you did everything perfect, there are simply so many things that can intervene to turn a good thing into a bad thing. A solid play call, no matter how well-schemed, no matter how sound, no matter how creative, can still end up being poorly executed, if not just out-defended by a great defensive player. Even if everybody does their job, you're still playing with a ball that's shaped like an egg. It just bounces funny. Simple physics can either play into your hands or can turn against you.

Winning and losing. It's a fine line. Much too close to be pass/fail, either a dog-pile success or an abject failure, with no ground in between.

You've got to keep things in perspective. To put it in football language, you can't let a single, isolated loss beat you twice. You can't let negative voices (either your own or other people's) be the only opinions that weigh in on how you did. Just as victories can sometimes hide weaknesses and mistakes that lurk underneath, losses can all too easily obscure a lot of good things that are happening as well, things you can build on for later.

In many ways, it just gets back to that commitment of keeping things simple. Let's say you come up against a decision in life that, as you debate how to handle it, your options aren't clear-cut. There are lots of variables and competing considerations that influence how you're going to respond. The difference between choosing well or guessing wrong is not that far apart. You pray about it. You want to do God's will. But even if you do your best to be faithful, you may end up not being so sure you made the right call.

I agree with God's Word that says, "If the eagerness is there, the gift is acceptable" (2 Cor. 8:12 CSB). God doesn't look on the outside; He looks on the heart. You go with what you've got, knowing your intention is to please Him, knowing He understands what you're dealing with.

So I just think God loves it when, after you've sorted through the clutter to figure out what He's leading you to do in a certain thing at work, or at home, or wherever, *you do it*. And if after all that, based on the early returns, it feels like a loss, a regret, or a goof-up, then just go back to where you started from. Go back to where your heart was situated when you made that call. Go back to how diligently you sought to perform your duty in whatever that moment required.

Be careful about trusting your feelings when they're making you feel like a failure, like a loser.

Be careful about trusting your feelings when they're making you feel like a failure, like a loser. They've been known not to tell the truth.

━━━

We were back in the SEC championship game for the second year in a row. We'd gotten clocked by LSU, 42–10, in the 2011 edition, despite roaring into it on a ten-game winning streak. Now it was 2012, and our regular season had been even more of a success. At 11–1, we'd risen to #3 in the country, making our matchup against #2 Alabama a *de facto* play-in game for a shot at the national championship. Notre Dame was the sole unbeaten team in college football that year, and by virtue of their independent status (meaning, they had no conference title game to play), they were already slotted into the BCS final. The winner of our game was for sure headed to Miami, to take them on, for all the marbles.

And this game was a knock-down, drag-out.

For all but the last two minutes of the first half, we kept the Alabama offense off the scoreboard. Eddie Lacey finally broke a forty-yard touchdown run with two minutes to play in the second. Then, following an interception on our next drive, they tacked on a go-ahead field goal to take a 10–7 lead into the locker room.

But we came out firing to start the third—a statement drive, consisting mostly of Todd Gurley runs, including a touchdown blast that put us back in front. Then came the first big turning-point break of the game: a blocked field goal, which our Alec Ogletree scooped up in stride and dashed fifty-five yards for another score. The Georgia lead, at the 6:30 mark of the third quarter, was 21–10. Even after they caught us to start the fourth, we answered with a long Aaron Murray pass to Tavarres King and another Todd Gurley power run into the end zone. New score: 28–25, in favor of the good guys.

And so, following a Bama punt, seven minutes and fourteen seconds was all the distance that separated our team from a shot at Georgia's first national championship in a generation. Even after a three-and-out, now with only *four* minutes left, we still led the game and had them third and five at midfield—the same exact spot where we'd stopped them dead on their previous possession a few minutes earlier.

But this time, we couldn't seem to corral their powerful running game. T. J. Yeldon slipped through a missed tackle, converting the first down by a hair. If not for that half-yard, the next play would likely have never been possible: A. J. McCarron's first-down, fifty-yard bomb to Amari Cooper that inched them back ahead, 32–28.

But our guys fought on, like warriors. We stalled, we punted, then we held them to three downs on their end of the field. It bled us of time-outs, but the defense at least gave Aaron a final crack at leading the offense into position. Starting on our own 15 with just over a minute to play, he cobbled together a hit-and-miss drive that appeared to be over when cornerback Dee Milliner dove to pick off a deflected pass. It was close. Hard to tell. But after a long review, the interception was overturned. The championship game was still within reach. Miami Gardens, at that moment, was a mere seventy-two yards from Atlanta.

Soon, it was only eight.

With fifteen seconds to do it.

How can *everything* and *nothing* be only eight yards and fifteen seconds apart?

━━━

I was not, um . . . I was not happy at the postgame press conference. Normally I got along well with the press. There were a lot of great people in the media, including one of our own, UGA grad Maria Taylor, who is now part of ESPN's *College GameDay* package, as well as their NBA coverage. Her first interview, I think, as a student, was interviewing me after practice on campus. But really, just about all the media I dealt with were fair and cordial. I always thought we had a good relationship.

I wasn't particularly pleased, though, with the line of questioning that came at me after this tough championship loss to Alabama.

Reporter: There are some people, whether it's fans, media, or whoever else that will maybe want to make further conclusions about you or your quarterback specifically in big games. Would you have any response to those people?

Me: I don't know what you're saying. Why don't you just say it straight up, what you're trying to say?

Reporter: There are people who will say that you and Aaron Murray specifically come up short on the biggest stage against the biggest opponents. Do you have any response to that?

Me: Is that what *you're* saying? Or are you trying to say everybody else . . .

Reporter: No, I'm saying that's what I hear every day on the radio.

Me: If that's what *you're* saying—are *YOU* saying that?

Reporter: No, I'm saying I hear it every day when I'm doing my job.

Me: Well, that's for you to worry about then. If that's what *you* say, then I'll answer the question. If you think *other* people are saying it—I'm not worried about that.

Yeah, I was aggravated, to say the least. Ticked. And even as I stood up hastily to walk away, I turned around and left a parting shot.

> **Me:** If anybody thinks our guys didn't play their
> tail off, and that Aaron Murray didn't play his
> tail off, they're crazy. I mean, that's unbelievable
> somebody would even bring that up.

I meant that. I *still* mean that.

Let me tell you something about Aaron Murray. I think this sums him up pretty well. When I took the head coaching job at Miami, I put together a series of teaching tapes (called "cut-ups") in order to help install and instruct players in the new offense I wanted to run. Cut-ups use actual game film to show how to run a variety of plays from your system, against this coverage, that coverage, or another coverage, against all kinds of different looks and blitzes. They're intended to teach you how to do it *right,* how to execute the plays correctly. And from all the clips that were available for me to choose from, across all fifteen years at Georgia, roughly 60–70 percent of those snippets featured Aaron Murray at quarterback. He did things so well. Just a great attention-to-detail kind of guy. Probably why he's the SEC career leader in touchdowns and passing yards. The numbers don't lie.

And so if you knew what solid quarterback play is supposed to look like, you saw it in Aaron during that Alabama game. And if you knew what you were looking for in quality football, you saw it in the players who were wearing *both* teams' helmets that night, not just the ones whose team was moving on to play Notre Dame.

The few seconds of the game that attracted the most scrutiny, of course, happened on the final play. Aaron threw the pass exactly as he should throw it against man-coverage—relatively low, relatively flat, where only the intended receiver in the end zone could make a play on the back-shoulder fade throw. Unfortunately the ball got tipped at the line, caroming directly to another receiver, Chris Conley, who was located around the 5—exactly where the play called *him* to be positioned as well.

The fact that knocking the ball down instead of catching it in that instance would've technically been the best option for him to take doesn't negate the fact that catching balls is what receivers instinctively do. You can't fault him for that. People faulted me as a coach for it—for having an eligible receiver standing anywhere on the field that wasn't the end zone—and yet he was serving a purpose by being there. His presence in the flat was designed to put the cornerback in conflict about who to cover. Under no circumstances was the pass to be thrown to him. It was going to Malcolm Mitchell the whole time—either with the back-shoulder fade against man-to-man coverage or with more of a lob pass, a jump ball, if the corner had been playing zone. But again, the ball was deflected near the line of scrimmage. Chris caught it, slipped, got tackled in-bounds, the clock ran out, and we couldn't get off another play.

It was a painful loss, to put it mildly. It was arguably a legacy loss, to state it broadly. If we'd won that game—which, again, we were only eight yards and fifteen seconds away from doing—we would've been in the BCS championship that Alabama won 42-14. You could therefore make the case that we would've beaten Notre Dame, too, since we'd played the same Alabama team to such a close finish. And—I know this is all hypothetical, but—if we had won the 2013 national championship, it's hard to imagine I would've been shown the door after continuing to post ten-win seasons in both 2014 and 2015, which we did.

You can't drive yourself crazy with it. You trust God to do what He alone knows is best. But you don't draw hard lines of winning and losing where He's only looking for your obedience and faithfulness. A lot of your losses may be victories in disguise.

18

Keep Calm

I f there's one comment I heard (and frankly still hear) more than any other, concerning how people saw me as a coach, I'd say it's in that vein of "doesn't show much emotion," "is always on an even keel," "steady," "quiet," "calm." Most people mean it as a compliment, I think.

Not everybody. I was once the featured villain of the Evict Richt Club, back when I was offensive coordinator at Florida State. Or that's what their so-called "president" would tell me, every time he called to leave a long, ranting message on voice mail. One day I decided just to answer the phone and let him talk, let him spew directly into my ear about whatever was stuck in his craw, about how we didn't run the ball enough to suit him or whatever. He wasn't content, I guess, with his team being top-five in America in scoring and in just about every other offensive category as well. I finally cut him off and said, look, "How about if I invite you over to the office one of these days after the season, we can sit down together, and you can ask anything you want to ask me." Turns out, critics aren't big fans of showing their own faces. I think that was the last I ever heard of him.

More often than not at Florida State, people's reasons for being mad at me came from games that we won but didn't win by enough. Not enough to cover the point spread. If I took a knee at the end of the game when we conceivably could've kept playing for another score, I would sometimes hear about it from guys who'd lost their lunch money gambling.

One time I picked up a message on our answering machine from someone who'd managed to get our home number. It started out, "If this is Coach Richt at Florida State University," followed by the filthiest, four-letter barrage of insults you can imagine. Then when he finally reached the end of his little tirade, he finished by saying, "If this is *not* Coach Richt, I'm sorry to bother you."

I had news for him. It didn't bother Coach Richt either.

Sometimes, though, the criticism could turn dangerous, or at least dangerous-sounding. A fifty-something guy claiming to be a Georgia fan dialed the number at the athletic office almost immediately after our 2005 home loss to Auburn by one point. Maybe you remember that game, the one where they hit on a long, fourth-and-ten pass in the last two minutes to set up a come-from-behind field goal. On the call, the man threatened to drive a van over to my house and beat me to death with a baseball bat.

Ordinarily we might've let it go, except that either the campus police or the GBI (Georgia Bureau of Investigation) traced the call to somewhere in Atlanta, where we ended up being scheduled to play in the SEC championship game a few weeks later. So to keep everybody safe, the state troopers who were in charge of protecting me tracked the guy down, appeared at his home, scared him senseless.

Apparently the whole thing had been a drunken reaction to the game in front of his friends. He'd been out of his head. But still it was an actionable threat that couldn't be ignored. We didn't press charges or have him arrested, but I'm sure having armed law officers show up at your door asking questions will go a long way toward changing your drinking habits.

Criticism, though, is just the nature of the beast in sports. Coach Bowden used to say, "If you can't handle criticism, you need to get out of coaching." The thing he told us to remember was that people's criticism is usually not personal; they're just aiming their anger at whoever the coach happens to be. He was right about that. It can *feel* personal sometimes, and certain people try to *make* it personal. But the minute I stopped coaching, most people, I noticed, suddenly didn't feel the need to tell me how to do my job. That's football for you.

> **People's criticism is usually not personal; they're just aiming their anger at whoever the coach happens to be.**

But they do still talk about the "calmness" thing.

So here's what I'd say to you about that. First, I'm from Nebraska. If you know anyone from Nebraska, good chance you don't think of them as being super animated. Being calm is just sort of our natural demeanor. We're not too gregarious in our gestures and tone, except maybe in our sarcastic sense of humor. We're just normally not very loud. We're calm people. That's who I am.

And I found in coaching, same as I think you'll find in every other walk of life, it's important to be true to who you are. I loved Coach Bowden, for instance, as you know, but when I became a head coach, I didn't need to try to *be* Coach Bowden, or to be any other coach that I admired or respected. Your players need to know you're real. They need to know you're genuine. Trying to be someone you're not is . . . first of all, it just takes too much energy. It's exhausting. It's a waste of your limited, inner resources. And, second, people will end up seeing right through you anyway. You can't maintain an act forever.

But in my case, staying calm on the sideline was more than just a demeanor. It was deliberate. I recognized, as far back as

my days as a play caller at Florida State, I made better decisions
if my mind wasn't racing. I couldn't think as clearly if I let myself
get too agitated or excited. I wasn't at my best if I was flustered.
So I would pray before each game, at every place I coached,
asking God to calm my spirit: "Please, Lord, help me to think
straight. Please help me to make good decisions today." I just felt
more in control if He was helping me stay self-controlled.

And I think when it comes to making decisions, that's good
counsel for all of us . . . even if you're not from Nebraska. The
Bible talks about letting the "peace of Christ rule in your hearts"
(Col. 3:15). To the extent that we do that, I believe we make more
reasoned, responsible decisions that are right for the moment,
for whatever challenges and dilemmas we're facing. Praying for
peace, for calmness—I think it just works.

But in football, of course, even a strength is subject to being
interpreted as a weakness. When we were winning big at Georgia,
my calmness was considered stoic. The steady, consistent play of
our team and of our quarterback was said to be an extension of
their coach's evenhanded touch, of his unflappable nature. Then
we'd lose a game or two, and the papers and phone lines would
fill up with how I didn't have any fire in the belly, how I didn't
exude the kind of energy needed to take a good team over the
top.

There we go with the criticism again.

You've just got to take it calmly.

——

One of the residual blessings of striving for calmness is
the opportunity to help others stay calm in their own stressful
situations. Midway through the 2015 season, after suffering
back-to-back losses to Alabama and Tennessee, we were
struggling at home against Missouri, grinding to a 6–6 tie with
about six minutes left to play. Our kicker, Marshall Morgan, after

a fourth-quarter drive stalled at the 8, trotted onto the field to attempt a twenty-six-yard field goal from the left hash, for the lead. The ball hooked left.

Kickers have it hard. They face a lot of pressure. Though they're part of a team effort like everyone else, the spotlight tends to rest on them individually, more than on most of the other players. Every play for them is a scoring play. That's why they feel singularly responsible for failing the team whenever they come up short, or wide, or off-line, or however else a kick can be missed.

So I was glad for Marshall when our defense held, turning the ball back over to our offense for a shot at giving him another chance. We moved inside our opponent's 20-yard line, fourth and three with 1:48 on the clock.

A Missouri time-out gave me a moment to catch him on his way onto the field. "Marshall," I said, with my arms resting on his shoulder pads, "whether you miss it or make it, you're still my guy, all right? I just want you to know I love you, no matter what happens."

I wish more people, football players in particular, could hear someone say that to them. When they're doing well, when their game is clicking, everything feels right in their world. They feel like they're earning their accolades. They're confident because they're succeeding. But the minute they experience a slipup or a setback, their whole mood and outlook can go in the tank.

Again, it goes back to identity. It goes back to that confusion between "what we do" and "who we are." You need to be a child of God (who you are) who happens to play football, or coach football, or teach school, or raise a family (what you do). The Bible talks about us being a "new creation" once we've given our lives to Christ (2 Cor. 5:17 csb)—people who, yes, are unhappy when we fail at what we do, but who can still rest in the encouragement of being who we are, regardless.

I was able to say the same thing to another of our players one day, not in a game situation but simply a game-of-life situation that was making him feel defeated, depressed, and despondent. His mother called me in the middle of the night, genuinely afraid after talking to her son that he might be at the point of taking his own life. I immediately called our team chaplain—my brother-in-law Kevin Hynes (better known as "Chappy"), my sister Mikki's husband—who, as he was always willing to do, rushed over to where this guy lived to see what was going on.

Early the next morning, Chappy brought him into my office. For several minutes I listened to this young man tell me how he was failing at everything he was trying to do with his life. "What do you mean by that?" I asked.

Well, he said, he'd gotten injured (which I knew, of course), and it was keeping him from being the ballplayer he wanted to be. He was also struggling in his classes. He was doing pre-med work, if I remember correctly, and some of the science courses were tangling him up in knots. To top it off, he said, he was failing as a Christian. He'd been giving into temptation with his girlfriend. He was doing things he knew weren't right. All these struggles and mistakes came spilling out in my office that morning in a gush of disappointments, telling me how he was letting everybody down—himself, his family, his team, his God.

"Let me ask you something," I said. "This sin you're committing with your girlfriend. Did you ever do that kind of thing before you became a Christian?"

"Yes."

"Did it use to bother you like this?"

"No."

"But now that you're a believer, it's making you miserable, right?"

"Yeah, it is."

"Hallelujah," I said. "That's a *good* thing." He looked at me like I was crazy. "No, see, you're a new creation now. God's Spirit lives inside you. You can't be comfortable sinning anymore. Thumbs-up," I said. "That's not failing; that's growing."

As Christians, the moment we agree with God that we are sinners in need of a Savior—the moment we put our faith in Jesus—we become right with God. The sin nature we're born with is "crucified with Him, in order that our body of sin might be done away with" (Rom. 6:6). We become a new creation in Christ.

As a result, because we've accepted the gift of Jesus' sacrifice for our sin, we are totally accepted by God. It's not that our sin just magically went away; it's that Jesus paid the price for it. *Someone* had to pay. And His death on the cross was the perfect price, the perfect sacrifice, because He, unlike us, had no sin to pay for. He was perfect. He chose, in love, to lay down His perfect life in our place. His death became the price we owe.

So when we believe in Him, the penalty due for our sin is paid in full. All our guilt, all our punishment, is taken away. We are free. Perfectly free.

But even though our spirits have been perfected, our behavior is still a work in progress. Unlike the immediacy of what happens when we receive Christ, the change in our behavior happens over time as we mature in our faith, as we daily begin to understand and experience the changed person God has made us to be. Our behavior (what we do) starts to line up with the new creation we've become in Christ (who we are). We start to behave better—not because we fear His judgment, but because we love Him for who He is and what He's done for us.

Again, it's a work in progress. But even though our behavior is not yet perfect, our spirit and soul already are. That's the best news in the world. And that's why we can have peace with God, because we have assurance of our salvation. We can rest from the burden of having to perform to get God's approval.

To put it another way: "You're my guy, Marshall, no matter what happens." Just go out there and kick the dang ball.

He did. We won.

Believers sometimes fail, but we are never failures.

We are loved as children of God. That's *who we are*.

=====

My first year at Georgia, I came face to face with the kind of unexpected challenges that can greet a head coach at any time, things that appear to have nothing at all to do with football. Ron Courson, our director of sports medicine, came barging into one of our staff meetings after a mid-season practice one Wednesday afternoon, and said, urgently, "Coach, you need to come downstairs."

One of our junior defensive lineman, David Jacobs, a guy with legitimate NFL-level talent, had lost consciousness in the locker room, had stopped breathing. Ron and the training staff had been able to resuscitate him, but he was being rushed by ambulance to the hospital. All signs pointed to a stroke.

A stroke? Were they serious?

I still remember the first time I went to see him. He was lying there in his hospital bed, trying to speak—alive, but otherwise incoherent. It just tore me up. To the best of my recollection, we were the only two people in the room at that moment, and I began praying over him, crying over him. I didn't think he could even hear me or know what I was saying. I found out later that he could, and did. All throughout his rehab, he and I became even closer. He fought every day—fought for his life with the same determination that he'd fought to play football at Georgia.

When the next season rolled around, in what would've been his senior year, he'd gotten himself strong enough to walk again, even to jog a little bit, although unsteadily. We'd put him on staff in sort of an assistant-coach capacity. It was good for him, and good for us, to still have him around, still helping out the ball team.

One day, toward the end of November, he stepped into my office and said, "Coach?"

"Yeah. What is it, David?" (Get ready for this.) He said, "Coach, do you think I could put on my uniform one more time?"

Man.

The last game of the year, 2002, was a home game against Georgia Tech. As usual, it was Senior Day, where all the senior players are introduced individually before the game. They run out onto the field with a sleeve of flowers to give to their mom or grandma, shake hands with the coach, get their picture taken as a family. Traditionally the players on Senior Day are announced and sent out in alphabetical order, but this year I made an exception.

The crowd went ballistic when the last player's name was called: "David Jacobs." There he stood. And here he came, dressed in full pads and his #99 jersey, huge smile on his face, jogging out to greet his family. It was special. That moment is part of a full scrapbook of mental images and memories from my time as head coach at Georgia, but I've got to tell you, it's up there near the top.

Every year since those events, David comes back to the senior awards banquet and personally gives the David Jacobs Award to a player who, according to the trophy's inscription, "portrays the courage to face adversity, the spirit to never give up the fight, the character to do it right, and the determination to finish the drill." You knew we'd get the "finishing the drill" in there some way.

But that's not all. Even now, every Father's Day, David Jacobs is among the first to hit me up with a call or text that morning.

(He also made me godfather to his firstborn, David Jr.) Actually, Father's Day is about the busiest action my cell phone gets all year long. I usually hear from, I don't know—twenty-five, thirty, forty, fifty former players by the time the day is over. There's just no way to measure the value of those relationships that God graciously enabled me to build over time.

I love those guys. Every one of them.

I was hard on them. Because I loved them.

I was patient with them. Because I loved them.

I wanted to win with them. Because I loved them.

Even when I had to discipline them, it was because I loved them.

One day prior to a game, somebody stuck a microphone in my face, asking me about one of the players that I'd suspended for that week. "How come he's not playing today?" the reporter wanted to know.

Easy, I said. "Because I love him."

When it came to disciplining the players, it was really similar to how we disciplined our children. I had three things in mind: (1) an element of *punishment*. For the players, it might involve getting up for a 5:00 a.m. workout or losing playing time. With our children, it might be (depending on their age) a swat on their rear end, a time-out, a grounding, or maybe taking away a privilege. The second element: (2) *education*. We would explain to them what they'd done and why it's wrong, and how doing it right would prove beneficial in their lives, even a blessing to them. The third element: (3) again, *love*. Let them know it's not personal. We weren't condemning *them*; we were correcting their behavior. It didn't change the fact that we loved them unconditionally.

Being under authority and obeying is a very important skill. For children, it might save their lives one day—like, if they were getting too close to the street, and their parent called out to tell them to stop immediately. When it came to our players, we were hopefully helping to keep them from making decisions that would be harmful to them, perhaps even extremely hard to overcome later in life.

I think God does the same with us. At times the discipline makes us uncomfortable, but He is educating us through His Word, through the correction, and He is showing us, by being willing to teach us, that He loves us. Unconditionally.

And showing us that we can change, that He can change us. Discipline can be effective on its own in changing behavior, but the truth is, only when our heart is changed does our behavior change. Consistent change happens when, instead of behaving out of fear of punishment, we desire to obey out of love. When you win your player's heart, when you win your child's heart—when God wins *our* hearts—that's when things get really good.

That's just the way we ran things. That's the way we went about our business. When it came to discipline, each player knew exactly how it was going to be. The same boundaries applied to everybody, from the walk-ons to the four-year starters to everybody in between. They all knew what the expectations were. I didn't want anybody caught off guard if they did something they knew they weren't supposed to do. It was all spelled out for them.

The basic team rules and regs weren't really that hard: be *on time*; be *prepared* (prepared for your classes, for your tutoring sessions, for your workouts in the weight room, for practice, for the game itself); be *respectful* (respectful to your coaches, to your fellow students, to the girls on campus, to police officers, to your teammates); and do your *best*, things like that. Simple. But guys clearly understood the consequences of non-compliance.

If a player became chronic in not following these standards, and if his conduct wasn't getting any better, I had him sign a contract, along with his parents, stating exactly what he'd been doing and what he needed to do to straighten it out. Otherwise, he might end up facing a suspension, having his aid and scholarship revoked, perhaps even being dismissed from the team. He knew it could happen; it had happened before. But he had a way out. And I loved that young man and his family enough to hold him accountable, both for facing it and for fixing it.

Even back when a player was first being recruited, when they were visiting campus, I'd tell them, "When you come to my office, if I invite you into that living room area back there, it means we'll be having a nice visit. If I ask you to sit out here at the table, it means we'll be talking business. But if I tell you to sit in that chair directly across the desk from me, it means you're in trouble." And as I'd sometimes need to remind them later, when I was warning them about things we'd been seeing, I'd say, "Don't let my calm demeanor—don't let the fact that I'm talking with you about this in a calm fashion—confuse you into thinking I'm not taking this seriously."

Some of them didn't respond well to that kind of discipline. As a result, some of them lost the privilege of being on our ball team. I hated when it came to that, because it's not what I wanted, either for them or for us. But more than once in the years since, I've had some of those same players call me up to say, "Coach, I appreciate you dismissing me from the team. I knew I needed to change. I finally got my act together."

That's what love does.

I think it was Wayne McDuffie years earlier, who was the offensive coordinator at Florida State when I was just starting out in my career, who said to me, "Richt, you know what your problem is? You care too much." Ha, maybe so. But I never minded being accused of that. I don't think that's a bad thing to be. In fact, I think it made me a better coach. That's why I tried to get better at it as I went along.

In 2002, for instance, we won the SEC championship, destroying Arkansas 30–3 in the title game. Musa Smith ran for a couple of first-quarter scores, and tight end Ben Watson caught a twenty-yard touchdown pass late to completely put the game on ice. We were then matched up against a 9–4 Florida State team in the Sugar Bowl. *That* was interesting. For me. I was a little sentimental about playing them. Being only two years removed from being with Coach Bowden and some of the other coaches, watching players I'd recruited and coached and loved during my time in Tallahassee, was a weird feeling. But when I saw Coach Andrews across the way, pacing the sidelines, sporting that scowl of his, under his ball cap, it felt like being back at one of our old scrimmages. It was *ON* now. Sentiments out the window.

We beat them, 26–13, to finish with a 13–1 record and the #3 ranking in the country. Again, this was the BCS era. The national championship came down to a single game, #1 versus #2, and after Oklahoma lost to Texas A&M earlier in the year, Miami and Ohio State held the top spots the rest of the season. Even if we'd gone undefeated, even if we hadn't lost to Florida by a touchdown, we would probably have been the odd man out at the end. Finishing third that year was about as high as they were likely to put us, the way things played out.

But still, a great accomplishment. A great team. A *championship* team. Georgia's first SEC title in football in twenty years.

Shortly after that, I started hearing about some of our guys selling their championship rings. It wasn't a large number of them, but it wasn't just one or two of them either. It was several. And it hurt me. I didn't like it.

Everybody had their reasons, of course. Somebody had offered them money for it—some dude who probably had designs to make more money on it himself, which I hated thinking about. I doubted it was going to go in that person's trophy case.

I felt like our players were being taken advantage of. But, you know, their parents may have been hurting, or the player may have had a baby to help take care of, and if selling that ring was one way to do something tangible for his family, that's what he felt like he needed to do.

And I get it now. I get the motivation behind it. I get it more than I got it then, to be honest with you, because I came down pretty hard on them at the time. Maybe harder than I should have. I just didn't understand how anyone could sell something that was a symbol of our hard work together, just to pay bills.

It's probably why, years later when I was being introduced as the head coach at Miami, explaining some of my coaching philosophy, I said, "Life is about relationships. Rings collect dust." I don't mean to say that symbols of team accomplishment are worthless. I still believe they're worth a lot. When I had those Georgia players each write me a page—not to say that what they did was wrong, but just to get them to articulate what it meant to be part of a special team that accomplished great things together—I did it from a point of sincerity. I wanted them developing a team-first, me-second attitude.

Listening to people, seeking to understand their situations and circumstances, is how all of us grow closer together.

But the many years of coaching have taught me that listening to people, seeking to understand their situations and circumstances, is how all of us grow closer together. Caring for people, caring for your players, caring for your coaches—I don't think you can overdo those things.

The winning in football is important. It is. Vitally important. I've got no problem with somebody wishing we'd won more games at Georgia, especially wishing that one or more of those wins had been for a national championship. So do I. That would've been sweet.

I would also say that by any reasonable measure, a winning record of nearly three to one (74 percent) over the course of fifteen seasons hardly adds up to a less-than-winning culture.

But as important as those numbers are, nowhere should it be said in college football that relationships come second. Both the winning and the relationships that you build with your players are, in my mind, equally important. I don't buy the notion that a coach can't succeed on Saturday and care deeply about his players' lives every day of the week. I'm okay with that being my lasting reputation. Winning *and* caring.

And, of course, I say all this in a calm tone of voice.

PART IV

THE MIAMI YEARS

19

Exits and Encores

nyone who coaches at the University of Georgia is keenly aware of the priority placed on beating Georgia Tech. And we did that. Out of the fifteen times we played them, we won all but two.

Still, one loss was apparently one too many.

We headed into the 2014 game with a 9–2 record, back in the top ten. Tech was 9–2 as well, coming off an impressive home victory against #18 Clemson. Paul Johnson's teams were always solid, always well-coached in that ground-oriented offense. His 2014 team was among his best.

But mistakes and missed opportunities cost us the game. Both of our star freshman running backs (Nick Chubb and Sony Michel) fumbled at the goal line in the first half. Canceling out one of those cough-ups, senior cornerback Damian Swann somehow ripped the ball out of a scrum at *our* goal line and took it the length of the field for a ninety-nine-yard touchdown.

They blocked a kick; we blocked a kick. We converted a fake field goal attempt; they recovered an onside kick. It was that kind of day.

In the end—or what we *thought* was the end—quarterback Hutson Mason connected with Malcolm Mitchell on a fourth-and-goal TD completion with only eighteen seconds left, putting us up by three, 24–21. Looked like we'd done just enough. All we needed now was to kickoff, cover it, and walk out with a win.

As a rule, I didn't like to take many chances when it came to special teams. For instance, back in the "Hobnail Boot" win from 2001, after Verron Haynes had caught the pass that put us up 26–24 over Tennessee with just a few seconds left, I opted not to kick the extra point, even though it would've increased our lead to a field goal. Instead I kept the offense on the field and had David Greene take a knee. I didn't want to risk a muffed snap or the ball getting blocked, giving them a chance to capitalize on a last-second mistake. I preferred our chances at covering the ensuing kickoff.

And I felt the same way at the end of this game against Tech. Play it safe. Minimize risk. I went to our special teams coach and said, "Let's squib it."

What I really meant to say—but didn't say—was that I wanted the kicker to bloop it. Kick it up high in the air, have it land at around their 20 or 25, where maybe an up-back or a guy who's usually a blocker would fair-catch it or, even if he tried to run it back, they wouldn't be able to set up a good return. But again, "pooch it" or "bloop it" were not the words I said. "Squib it" is what came out of my mouth.

"Are you sure that's what you want?" he asked, a little haltingly.

"Yeah," I said.

"All right, Coach. That's what we'll do." I should've known right then, from the hesitation in his voice, that there was something amiss in our communication.

He told the kicker to squib it. Just like I said. The ball skittered and squirted along the ground, bouncing up conveniently to one of their return men at around the 30, who was able to advance it another fifteen yards. They now had the ball at their own 43, trailing by only a field goal, with thirteen seconds to go. I had just accidentally given them a second chance. A chance at one desperation play.

But our pass coverage held up. We rushed only three, giving quarterback Justin Thomas nowhere to go with the ball . . . except to carry it himself, twenty yards and out-of-bounds at our 37, leaving them four seconds on the clock to attempt a fifty-four-yard field goal. A slight breeze at his back, Harrison Butker's kick narrowly cleared the crossbar—his longest of the year. We were tied.

After that, not even a blocked extra point in overtime proved to be enough good fortune for us to salvage a win. Hutson's attempt to hit Malcolm again on a quick slant into the end zone, during our side's overtime possession, resulted in a game-ending interception.

Man, did that loss sting. Because we had it won. I mean, obviously the outcome of any game is never confined to just one play, no matter how devastating. Plus, you can never know, even if we'd kicked it deep, or at least deeper, whether they would've still returned it for a big gain. For a touchdown even. Nor did we have to let their quarterback scramble anywhere near field goal range, once we had him bottled up.

But what hurt the most, for me, was that it had come down to a matter of semantics. Of saying one thing while meaning another. The loss seemed so avoidable, if only I'd have been more careful about what I said. That was the worst part.

———

I want to break in here for just a second to talk about the power of our words.

Back when I was a quarterbacks coach, or even a coordinator, I was free to bust chops with the kids and just have fun. Being quick with the sarcasm is sort of the Richt Way. It's my natural personality. But I remember noticing early in my time as head coach at Georgia that the same kind of remarks, even if made in total playfulness, were often received as intentional digs. Guys would get their feelings hurt because the head coach was picking at them on the field. I usually meant it in a fun way, but they tended to hear it in a cutting way.

Then of course there was the media. Even in a blissfully Twitterless world, the things I might say in an interview or in an off-the-cuff moment could be diced and dissected, twisted into meaning something I never intended. You really had to guard your words. You never knew which ones might end up developing a life of their own.

But in reality, when I talk about every person being a *leader* in some form or fashion, the rules regarding being mindful about what we say apply to everyone. Each of us has influence. Our words have influence. We can use them to help or to hurt, to build up or tear down. "Death and life are in the power of the tongue," the Bible says (Prov. 18:21). It's up to us whether we use them well or not.

Parents, for example. If you're a parent, you have ongoing, repeated opportunities for helping to shape the way your child or children think about themselves. All of us can look back on things our parents said to us and how those words impacted our lives, either blessing us or making it harder on us. Words are powerful. They can carry enormous weight.

Coaches too. The first time my seat had started to become fairly hot at Georgia was in 2010, our only losing season. (There's a website dedicated to ranking the heat beneath individual "Coaches' Hot Seats," and I was definitely in the red.) But I was determined to keep the mood positive around our players, all the way down to the words I said.

I assigned them a book to read that offseason: *The Energy Bus* by motivational speaker Jon Gordon. It's a parable about a disgruntled guy whose car breaks down, forcing him to take the bus to work, only adding to his long list of troubles. But the upbeat demeanor of the bus driver is so infectious, it changes the man's whole perspective on things. Words and attitude matter.

So *The Energy Bus* mentality was pervasive in our building that year. We were going to stay positive. If a player was being what Jon calls in his book an "energy vampire," someone whose mouthing or complaining is proving toxic to the culture, we would superimpose that player's face on a vampire graphic that appeared on the television screens throughout the facility. Nobody wanted to be that.

Of course, *one* way to pump the positivity and get my fanny off the hot seat would be to put together some impressive wins to start the 2011 season. The schedule gave us the opportunity. We opened in the Georgia Dome against #5 Boise State, followed the next week at home against #12 South Carolina.

We lost them both.

The same guys who came up to me at church on the Sunday after our first loss, saying, "Coach, we're praying for you," came up to me on the Sunday after our second loss and said, "Coach, we're fasting for you." I said, "Things must really be bad out there."

I remember well the dynamic when I walked into the locker room after the South Carolina game. The narrative that had been building for months, the narrative we'd worked hard to change and counteract, had gotten a whole lot louder after this second straight week of losses. Coaches were starting to worry about their jobs. Players were starting to get ugly things said about them on the internet. And, of course, I was feeling as rotten as everybody.

But as the leader, I had a choice to make with my words. I chose to speak life into our team. Your words have that potential. Instead of marching in there and ripping their performance, I told them I felt encouraged, that I'd seen a lot of good things on the field that day. We basically won the statistical battle; we just didn't win the game. Like I mentioned before, we may have been 0–2, but we really weren't that far away from being 2–0.

I told them I believed in them. I told them I believed in what we could still accomplish. And by the end of that season, the headlines had gone from "Who's Going to Replace Coach Richt?" to "Coach Richt Receives Contract Extension." After those opening two losses, we reeled off ten straight wins, winning the SEC East.

Don't ever believe words aren't powerful.

"He who restrains his words has knowledge," the Bible says, "and he who has a cool spirit is a man of understanding" (Prov. 17:27). *A cool spirit.* I like that. Calm in our character; careful in our communicating. By recognizing and understanding the gravity of our words, we're living out a simple yet profound truth of life, one that we're wise to keep always in front of us.

That's honestly the mind-set I took into my final press conference at Georgia, the one where athletic director Greg McGarity formally announced that they were moving on from me and looking to hire my replacement.

There wasn't anything I could do about it now. He'd made his decision, and I had to live with it. But even on my way out, I wanted to honor God with how I presented myself. I wanted to show how a Christian man handles this type of situation. From the look on my face to the words that I said, I prayed I'd be able to communicate some important things that would stick with the people who were there and the ones who were watching.

I'd known it was coming, tracing all the way back to that Georgia Tech loss from the year before. We'd posted another respectable season in 2015, despite losing to the likes of Alabama and Florida. It didn't help my cause that we struggled to defeat a scrappy Georgia Southern team in overtime, or that we allowed Georgia Tech to play us close, since they'd come into that final game with only a 3–8 record. So, my firing wasn't a surprise. It didn't shock me. When the AD wants to talk to you on Sunday after your last game of the season, he's not likely wanting to discuss giving you a raise or a contract extension.

I would describe that private meeting as being short and not so sweet. I didn't say much. Kept a "cool spirit," I hope. I let him speak his piece, I shook his hand, and I left the room. By the next morning, I was seated beside him on a platform with a microphone in front of me, thankful for the opportunity to make a summary statement about the blessings of having been the Georgia coach for fifteen years.

I was thankful, too, that I'd gotten the chance to talk with my players as a team the night before. As I said to the gathered media that day . . .

> **Me:** I just wanted to help them understand that things like this can happen. It's part of the business. I encouraged them, number one, to behave . . . to stay accountable to everything we've always held them accountable to, academically and socially and all those things. But to also realize that they're basically making a first impression for their new head coach, starting yesterday.

So, yeah, I was glad for the chance to tell them face to face to "do the right thing and make a good first impression before you even meet whoever it is, and then be supportive of him," because "the faster everybody buys in," I said, "the better it's going to be."

Me: The last thing I asked them was to finish the bowl season great. We've got a bunch of seniors that are shooting for their fortieth win as a class. That's kind of hard to do. I know it means a lot to those guys.

"Finish the drill," in other words. To the end.

That moment with the players was extremely special. Even after it was over, after I'd finished speaking, it seemed like almost every guy waited around to come shake my hand or give me a hug. It was a long goodbye. I'll carry that memory always.

The players. It's really all about the players. And I had so many great players at Georgia. By one standard, you can quantify their caliber by the number of draft choices that came out of the program during those years—ninety-six in all, if you limit it to players I coached for at least one season. Sixteen of them were first-rounders: offensive linemen George Foster and Isaiah Wynn; defensive linemen Charles Grant, Jonathan Sullivan, and David Pollack; linebackers Jarvis Jones, Alec Ogletree, Leonard Floyd, and Roquan Smith; defensive back Thomas Davis; receivers Ben Watson and A. J. Green; running backs Knowshon Moreno, Todd Gurley, and Sony Michel; and quarterback Matt Stafford.

But draft status alone is hardly the only measure for the dozens, the hundreds of outstanding young men who played on those ball teams. What a privilege to have had, and to *still* have in many cases, such a wonderful relationship with so many guys who continue to make a difference in the world as Georgia football alumni.

Of course, a lot of the questions I fielded during the press conference that day were directed toward my future plans, wanting to know if I saw myself continuing to coach somewhere and, if so, when.

Me: There may be more opportunities that come in the next twenty-four to forty-eight hours, that type of thing. I'm going to listen to anyone who has interest in me. But since 1986, I've always tried to walk daily with the Lord and try to figure out what He wants me to do, and I try to be really obedient to that.

I was reading Matthew a couple of weeks ago, where Christ was praying before He was crucified, and was sweating blood. And He said, "Lord, take this cup from me. *Please* take this cup from me." He prayed that three times. And every time after He prayed that, He said, "Not my will, Lord, but thy will be done."

That's kind of been in my thoughts over the last couple of weeks, just, "Lord, Your will be done. Whatever Your will is, that's what I'll do." I just don't know what it looks like yet.

But I did know this . . .

Me: As I've said before, I just want God's will for me. I'm really at peace that this was part of His plan. I'm excited about what's coming down the road, and I want to continue to try to be as obedient as I can be to the Lord, and we'll see what He has in mind for Katharyn and me.

Bottom line? Yes, I would've loved to stay at Georgia for the rest of my coaching career. No doubt. But it didn't work out that way.

Me: I guess it's a lot like how I manage things in the middle of a game. If things don't go exactly the way you want—and you know they *don't* always go the way you want—you can spend a lot of time trying to figure out what happened or who did what. Or you can figure out where you are and what you need to do next to win. . . .

I feel the same way right now. I see where I am, Georgia sees where they are, and everybody's going to do what they think they need to do to have success in the future. So that's how I look at it.

And that's still how I look at it. Katharyn and I are thankful—thankful we had fifteen years in a wonderful place to raise our family. We did a lot of great things there, we have a lot of great memories from there, as well as a lot of great friends from there. I might've wished it had ended differently than it did, but I wouldn't change a word that I said on my last day there in red and black. Thankful, blessed, and wanting God's best. Wanting His will and nothing less. Both for myself and for UGA.

———

But I was tired. *Really* tired.

And my plan, from the moment I realized I was officially out at Georgia, was to do nothing for a year. Just sit back, rest, and recharge. The schedule that a college head football coach keeps is unbelievable. Unsustainable, really, in a lot of ways.

But within twenty-four hours of being let go—just as I was imagining how nice it might be for the first time in thirty some-odd years not to be out on the road recruiting—upward of six schools contacted me to see if I had any interest in coaching their football team.

Simply put, we'd just never been in this position before. Katharyn and I were trying to figure it all out on the fly. Our first inclination, simply because the volume had grown to so many, was that we should at least listen, see what they had to say. But before the end of the first day, I think, we'd decided not to let the madness dictate. We were pretty sure we just needed some time off. So it didn't seem right, didn't seem fair, to waste everybody's time. The only school we decided to consider, among those who'd reached out to us, was Miami. And if after we'd listened, if everything felt right, we'd be in. *All* in. Or we'd be out.

People think I was drawn to the Miami job because that's where I went to school and played ball. That's not really true. The fact that Miami is my alma mater was important but was not the main attraction. The fact that (1) they had an excellent recruiting base in south Florida, (2) you could win quickly there, (3) they already had a tradition of winning big there before, and (4) history can and does tend to repeat itself—those were the things that were on the forefront of my mind as I weighed the decision. Once we were *there,* once I'd settled into the job and had again become heavily invested in the Hurricane program, my longstanding ties to the school grew to mean even more to me, every day.

So, very quickly I realized I was attracted to it. Energized by it. Perhaps in a way that I didn't think I would feel about any other place. And since my window of time for accepting it wouldn't afford me a year off to catch my breath—since the Miami job wouldn't be open again for several more years, at a minimum—it was now or never, if that's where we wanted to go.

We did it.

And we did it very happily. Sort of like a new adventure. Where before, when we went to Georgia, we'd gone as a family, this time it was just Katharyn and me. (I did hire my son Jon to coach quarterbacks, but . . . he wouldn't be trailing along beside me on the sideline now, holding my cords.) My wife and I were looking forward to doing this one alone.

It was a fresh start. And it felt good. Getting back to basics.

Getting back to under-the-hood coaching.

> **Me:** I'll say this: If and when I do coach again, I'm
> looking forward to coaching in terms of being
> more hands-on. I miss coaching quarterbacks;
> I miss calling plays; I miss that part of it. . . . I'd
> be really excited about coaching QBs again and
> getting in the middle of coaching offensive strat-
> egy. Not that I wasn't in it, but I wasn't calling it.
> And I think I'd be more apt to do that again.

Good decision? Bad decision? My decision.
I was sure I could live with it.

20

The Meaning of Manhood

Between 1983 and 2001—a span of only eighteen years—the Miami Hurricanes were national champions five times, quarterbacked by the likes of Bernie Kosar, Vinny Testaverde, Steve Walsh, Gino Toretta, and Ken Dorsey. That's a couple of Heisman Trophy winners in there, surrounded by an incredible cast of players on both sides of the ball.

Hardly a year elapsed during that roughly twenty-year stretch when there weren't six or eight players, sometimes as many as ten or eleven, selected in the NFL draft, many of them in the first round. Among the highest draft picks: Alonzo Highsmith, Bennie Blades, Michael Irvin, Cleveland Gary, Cortez Kennedy, Russell Maryland, Warren Sapp, Ray Lewis, Edgerrin James, Santana Moss, Reggie Wayne, Ed Reed, Clinton Portis, Jeremy Shockey, Andre Johnson, Willis McGahee, Sean Taylor, Vince Wilfork . . .

See, I shouldn't have even started. They're almost too many to mention.

And whether warranted or not, those of us who played in the years leading up to Miami's ascent to the top of the college football world—like me, from 1978–1982—enjoy thinking we sort of set the table for the level of success that immediately followed.

But walking back onto the football facility in Coral Gables in December 2016, I was disappointed in what I saw.

One of my first, most telling observations was the sight of a golf cart parked raggedly along the side of the athletic building. It had once been utilized, I assumed, for ferrying recruits from one place to another during official visits. But on this day it just sat there, grass growing up around it, as if it had been there for quite some time, rocked to one side on a flat tire. Not from picking up a nail inadvertently on the sidewalk. The tread was worn down to the steel. The inner tube showed. This tire hadn't gone accidentally flat overnight. A deflation like that is a process. It takes time. Surely someone should have known it was about to pop and would do something about it, before the grass completely covered the darn thing.

Yet it was pretty much representative of what I saw, to be frank, looking around the facilities for the first time in a long time. I couldn't help noticing, for example, how the team records and bowl game victories and so forth, commemorated on the walls inside, had stopped being updated around seven or eight years ago, with no one bothering to refresh them. The phrase that came into my head was "The Land That Time Forgot." Like, did anybody care? Did anybody give a rip about this place anymore? It hurt to see that.

Because, remember—*five* national championships. Glittering success and superstars. A college football powerhouse on America's center stage.

How could it look like this underneath?

Of course, I knew the Miami culture from having played there, as well as from having coached at their most hated rival to the north, Florida State, so I can give you part of the answer. For one thing, Miami is actually a rather small and private institution.

A lot of people don't know that. Current enrollment, I believe, is around 11,000 students, which is far less than the 40,000-plus of a Florida or Florida State, or the 37,000 at Georgia. So it just doesn't have the giant alumni base. It doesn't launch 10,000 new graduates into the world every year. It doesn't have that huge endowment for athletics that many other schools possess.

And so whether from financial reality or just Miami cool, the mentality for a long time was, "Hey, we're winning big *without* all the fancy facilities and stuff. So why build them? We don't need them." Besides, they had more than enough athletes to recruit from the south Florida area who wanted to play there. Just sit back and let it happen. Watch us do it again, do it *our* way.

But at some point, the world grew smaller. Area kids and high school coaches started to hear and see what other places had, with their swanky indoor practice complexes and their sports psychologists and their in-house nutritionists and all, and pretty soon they were leaving home for the Alabamas and Oklahomas, going to play for schools in the Big 10 or on the West Coast. So gradually the talent pool around Miami started shrinking. Recruiting became more of an effort, more of a challenge. The result was a relatively meager run through the mid-2000s and 2010s, as Hurricane football gravitated from the old Big East to the new ACC and found themselves treading water in the Coastal Division. Barely .500 ball, with a few ticks upward every now and then.

But following a 58–0 home loss to Clemson midway through the 2015 season, the tires were deemed to have officially fallen off. The head coach was fired, the rest of the season played out, and the hunt was on for the next chapter, right as my own final chapter was being written for me at the University of Georgia.

Yet where my eyes saw flat tires, my heart saw opportunity. I was introduced with the hope of a new day at Miami, hopefully a return to the glory days.

I'd learned a lot in fifteen years of head coaching. The difference between forty-year-old Mark Richt showing up in Athens fresh out of the offensive coordinator's chair, and fifty-five-year-old Mark Richt showing up at Miami with experience in dealing with every kind of issue imaginable, both football and non-football . . . no comparison. I wasn't down on the carpet in my hotel room, wondering what I'd just done, I can tell you that. I knew exactly what I was getting into. I knew it was going to involve some heavy lifting, but I wasn't afraid of it. Katharyn and I, out on our own, were sailing right into it.

That's why only a couple of weeks after being hired, I was out to dinner with a couple of my old college teammates: Don Bailey, currently the radio analyst on Hurricane football broadcasts, and Ed Hudak, now the chief of police for Coral Gables, where the university is located. After dinner I drove them over to campus, parked at the baseball diamond, and we got out and walked to the practice field area just beyond it.

"Right here," I said, "is where we're going to build an indoor practice facility"—the one that people had been wanting and talking about for thirty years but had never been able to get off the ground. We had to have it. We were *going* to have it. I told them which direction the building would face, what it would sort of look like, the kind of grass we'd install for the playing surface, as well as the various rooms and meeting spaces that would go all around it—weight room, locker room, video rooms, coaches' offices.

I hadn't come to be a caretaker. I'd come to change things. I couldn't do it myself, of course. Thankfully I had Blake James, athletic director, and Jenn Strawley, deputy director of athletics, to help me, along with lots of other people, doing lots of work, investing lots of support. But I was determined to lead. I was determined to build. To coach and counsel and care for a group of guys who would be part of getting Miami football back on the rails again.

That's what men are made to do. To take care of business.

======

Each offseason, either in the spring or summer, I always made a point of leading our players in some kind of Character Ed emphasis. I'd done it ever since I became a head coach. Sometimes guys would say (or I could tell they were thinking), "Why are we doing this? It's not helping us win football games." No, I believe it does. I believe the better man you build, the better team you have. I really do. I'd seen it happen. And besides that, I loved these guys. I cared about them. I knew and loved their families as well, and I knew part of the reason they entrusted their sons and grandsons to us was to help develop their character at this critical phase of their lives.

A lot of their parents would say to me, especially the single mothers, "I can teach him a lot of things, Coach, but I can't teach him how to be a man. I need you to do that for me." And I took that charge to heart. I believed my job as a college coach had as much to do with growing good men as with growing good football players. If all we do is teach them how to block and tackle, how to throw and catch, we've failed them as coaches in the college ranks. We've done them a disservice. Whenever their moms and dads would say, "He's all yours now, Coach," and I would feel what I felt in my heart as they said it, I knew God had called me not only to be a football coach but to be a coach of college-age young men. To help them become tomorrow's men.

> I believed my job as a college coach had as much to do with growing good men as with growing good football players.

"Manhood" was the theme I wanted to talk about in the 2017 offseason. But prior to that summer, my second year on the job, I was having a hard time finding what I was looking for, in terms of a memorable approach to manhood, a working definition that I thought our guys could relate with and strive toward. I finally found it on YouTube in a sermon by Dr. Tony Evans, senior pastor of Oak Cliff Bible Fellowship in Dallas, Texas, and former chaplain of the Dallas Cowboys and the NBA's Dallas Mavericks.

A lot of people, athletes in particular, equate manhood with being macho, with having an aggressive sort of pride in their masculinity. And for football players and front-line soldiers and even fathers raising their families, it is important to be fierce enough to fight for and defend the things you care about. God gives men testosterone for a reason. But true manhood is not determined by what you can bench press or how many women you can impress. Dr. Evans described it as a progression that all men are meant to make through three *'hoods,* he calls them. And I'm thankful for his permission to adapt it here in print.

The first "hood" is *malehood.* Malehood is simply your sexual identity. Your gender. The particular body parts you're born with. The ones that make you different from a female. The second is *boyhood,* which he describes as being marked by immaturity, irresponsibility, and a high level of dependence on somebody else to take care of you. And though each of these terms sounds negative when you first hear them, there's nothing wrong with being a little immature, irresponsible, and dependent on others if you're a kid. It's merely a part of what we all work through when we're boys.

But here's the problem, I said to our team that summer. It's okay to be a boy when you're five or six or seven or eight— immature, irresponsible, dependent—but not when you're twenty-eight, thirty-eight, forty-eight. You get me? That's when it's time to be living in the third hood. *Manhood.*

In manhood, Dr. Evans says, you take care of business. You do your job, whatever it is. You own your responsibilities, whatever they are. Speaking of responsibility, for instance, I chose to add a fourth hood: *fatherhood,* because that's one of the things I really wanted to talk with our players about. We all know the glaring statistics that mushroom-cloud around children from fatherless homes: the poverty, the behavioral problems, the substance abuse, the suicides. It's undeniable. It's beyond debate. Cold, hard, *desperately* hard facts. The kind of facts I felt responsible not only for sharing but hopefully preventing.

Because just being a male, I told them, and just having the required plumbing to become a father, doesn't yet make you a man. You can find yourself in the fatherhood stage without having ever left the boyhood stage. And what do boys tend to do when they're faced with responsibility? They run from it. Boyhood-dwelling fathers do that. Maybe their *own* father did that.

And so, we just talked about how, basically, no matter where you were born (when you first experienced malehood), and no matter what kind of family you grew up in (the one where you experienced boyhood), you still have a decision to make. A call to make. About becoming a man. About entering manhood. Growing beyond immaturity, irresponsibility, and dependence.

It brings to mind a conversation I had with Michael Irvin, the Dallas Cowboy great of the 1990s. His son was on our team at Miami during my years there, and I had needed to exercise some discipline on him because of a couple of things Michael Jr. was doing. Nothing terrible, but just some stuff that needed correcting. Michael didn't rush to defend his kid or make excuses for what he'd done. "I sent him to you as a boy; I want him back as a man," he said to me. "Squeeze the boy until a man comes out."

I love that. "Squeeze the boy until a man comes out." Every player who came to our program in the "boyhood" stage should leave our program in the "manhood" stage.

And if they would commit to making that decision themselves, I told them—if you determine today that when you get married you will love your wife the way Christ loved the church, being willing to lay down your life for her, and if you will take responsibility for loving and blessing and providing for your children, the way God our Father models for us, you will start a chain reaction. Your daughter will grow up knowing what to look for in a real man. Your son will grow up knowing what it means to be a loyal, faithful, loving husband and father. And when their children come along—your grandchildren—those kids will grow up knowing the same thing. Within a few generations, the decision you make today, I said, could potentially affect hundreds of people's lives. All because you—you!—this one guy, you!—stepped up into manhood.

Nothing excites me more than to hear that one of my former players is loving his wife and children the way Christ loves the church. Living out what it means to be a true man. God's kind of man!

Men, lead your homes. There's power in that.

Power in making the call of responsibility.

=====

My main responsibility at Miami, just like my main responsibility at Georgia, was to win football games. No question. I love winning football. But football, even a winning brand of football, is no more than a four- or five-year slice of life for the players who pass through your program. That's it. And after that for them, it's out into the woods with the wolves of the real world. Part of my job was to get them ready for it.

And so we'd bring people in from time to time, usually early in the spring or summer, in the offseason, to talk about résumé writing, and networking, and dressing for a job interview, and using the right fork at a restaurant. Life skills, as opposed to just football skills.

But most of the players weren't ready to listen to all that. They were tired. They'd been lifting. They'd practiced. They'd run. And anyway, they were going to the NFL. They'd have a million dollars to help figure all that out, if they ever needed to.

But the vast majority of them, even if they did get to sniff a pro football practice field, would never suit up for a single down. It's hard to make the league. Even if you do, the average career is no more than three-and-a-half years. The odds are against you. I knew it firsthand. In fact, maybe that's why God took me through those years of failing and being fired, of getting cut and carrying my playbook again to the coach's office. He gave me a heart for how it feels to be on the other side of football, to not know which way is up. Or if *any* way is up.

But after a while, it felt as though just having a heart for them wasn't enough. I'd become accustomed to having my phone ring, to talking with yet another player who'd been cut from an NFL roster and didn't know what to do with his life. "Coach, can you help me?" We always did what we could, but I knew we needed to do more. We needed to get more organized. We needed to be more streamlined.

We established at Georgia what we called the P.O. Network, in memory of one of our former players, Paul Oliver, so that whenever the next player called me, needing help going forward in life, there would be people already in place where they could be directed. Travis Butler and other business leaders in the area helped facilitate the initiative. Friends of the program and former players who'd become successful could reach out with a steady, helping hand, becoming the mentors these young guys really needed at a crossroads moment. We put a similar program together at Miami, called the U Network, based on the exact same model. And initiating it was as important to me as anything else we were working to accomplish with our ball team. Thanks to the help of Stuart Miller and Darin McMurray, we got it done, helping many former players find work.

Community service was important to me too. During my time at Miami, we actually led the nation—#1 among all FBS schools—in the number of hours our players gave to helping people in need. I'd bring in area leaders to talk with our team, maybe as many as five over the course of the offseason, discussing various projects that we could get involved with. Then I'd ask the players, out of those five options, to pick two they wanted to do. (I didn't tell them I wasn't actually able to mandate that they participate, by rule. I just told them to sign up.)

I knew, like you surely know, how helping somebody who can't help you back will adjust your whole perspective. Getting our players out there, where they could see that the world didn't revolve around them, or around football, and that they could find joy in giving to people, was huge in their lives. I wanted them to experience that for themselves.

Call it responsibility. Simple as that. It's not something I deserve any credit for. It's just part of what God put men on this earth to do. Manhood equals responsibility.

> **Helping somebody who can't help you back will adjust your whole perspective.**

So when I say that deciding to take the Miami job didn't have a lot to do with it being my alma mater, but that after I became the head coach my alma mater became more important to me, the thing it inspired in me was responsibility. Which surprised me a little, frankly. I didn't expect to feel such a deep, immediate sense of duty and obligation. To my school.

But in cooperation with Blake James and others in the Miami administration and universe, I became determined to implement a vision for greatness in the Hurricane football program. That's why I poured myself into getting that indoor facility out of the south Florida sand, even giving a million dollars of Katharyn's and my own money to go toward its construction.

Obviously, again, I needed a lot of help. The Carol Soffer Indoor Practice Facility would not be there today without the incredible generosity and support of the Soffer family. I think it's cool, too, that such a major piece of the athletic landscape on the Miami campus is named for a woman. I know that means a lot to Carol as well. It also stands for the hundreds of boosters and former players and people in the athletic department who put skin in the game to make it a reality. But it was time, when I came there as coach, to start getting serious about putting together the team that could get that glaring need of the football program off the wish list and into the list of reasons why kids wanted to come to Miami.

Responsibility.

It's also why I allowed my contract to be rewritten—reduced by several hundred thousand dollars—so that some of the money that was supposed to come to me would go instead into a fund to increase the salaries of my coaching staff, to give them the raises they deserved for their commitment to Miami, to keep them from being cherry-picked by other schools.

Responsibility.

It's why we put the following words together as our coaches' mission statement, and anchored them in the wall so that all of us could stay reminded of it:

Handle all responsibilities with excellence.

Be dedicated in assisting our players to reach
their full potential in the classroom, on the
football field, and in society.

Help them develop their body, mind, and spirit
to the fullest.

Be a great example of what we are trying to
teach our players.

Do not do anything that would destroy what we
are trying to build.

Honor God with all of our actions.

Truthfully, if all we did was the last line, that's all we really needed—to honor God with our actions. That's not just what responsibility says; it's what it does.

It's what manhood does.

To be honest, I've been a little uncomfortable writing this chapter, because I know it might read a bit like a Mark Richt commercial. That's not my intention, I promise you. All I'm trying to say is this: *men are made for responsibility*. And even if you've reached the age where you've already raised your kids, maybe put them through college, where you're established and settled and experienced in your career, it's not time to sit back, count your money, and live off of your past accomplishments. It's time to be challenged by the new responsibilities of the moment. It's time to avoid slouching back into boyhood, the temptation to take your foot off the gas and rest it on your footstool.

Paul said, "When I was a child, I used to speak like a child, think like a child, reason like a child; when I became a man, I did away with childish things" (1 Cor. 13:11). What might be a new responsibility that God is even now calling you to step up into? Maybe that's a call you need to make.

It won't just make you *feel* like a man; it's how you and I become and live as real men.

21

Over and Out

H ard Rock Stadium was rocking that night.

ESPN College GameDay had brought their traveling road show to town, and Miami fans were into it like it was 1989. Maybe even more into it. To hear the old-timers talk, the atmosphere at this game was a throwback to how they remembered things used to feel during those high-flying years at the old Orange Bowl. Home games had moved from there in 2008, twenty miles from campus to the home of the NFL Dolphins, and most of the games in most of those years had felt cavernous by comparison.

Not tonight. A-Rod and J-Lo were in the house, along with a capacity crowd of 65,000, as we were set to take on the Notre Dame Fighting Irish—8-1 and #3 in the nation—in a battle that was thick with postseason implications. Though undefeated, we were three-point underdogs at home, sitting at #7 behind three one-loss teams, Notre Dame included. A win tonight would launch us into the top-four playoff discussion.

Truth of the matter, our 8-0 record could realistically have been 9-0, had we not been forced to cancel a game against Arkansas State in early September because of the threat of Hurricane Irma. Still, our winning streak dating back to the previous season currently stood at thirteen. Of the four teams who'd beaten us in 2016, we'd already beaten three of them this year—Florida State and North Carolina, as well as Virginia Tech a week earlier in convincing fashion, 28–10. The fourth domino was now within reach tonight, the team who'd come from behind last year to nip us by a field goal at South Bend.

We were pumped.

And took care of business.

The rout was on early, leading to a 41–8 runaway win. Coach Brian Kelly inserted redshirt freshman Ian Book at quarterback midway through the second, seeking a spark, but the Turnover Chain kept showing up around our guys' necks. (Turnover Chain? You know what that is? The heavy, gold, Cuban-link neckwear with the massive "U" at the bottom was meant to spur defensive players into forcing opponents into mistakes. It had been the inspiration of defensive coordinator Manny Diaz. Anyone who picked off a pass or recovered a fumble was honored with wearing it, to the delight of our fans, the moment he got to the sideline.) The chain ended up making four dramatic appearances that night against Notre Dame, including the knockout punch when Trajan Bandy jumped the rout on a little flare to the right of the formation and hauled it sixty-five yards for a halftime-ending, 27–0 lead.

It was just one of those games when everything went right. The whole day went right. The whole week had gone right. We woke up Monday morning, following the rest of the college football action around the country, as the #2 team in the nation.

The U was making waves again.

———

Man, was it exciting being part of the resurgence of Miami Hurricane football.

But it had definitely taken a toll on me.

On my body. On my energy. On my inner reserves and resources.

Katharyn and I, as I said, had come to this job with a completely all-in mentality. We could see all the things that were needed. We knew the massive amount of time and effort it would require. In addition, of course, I'd gotten the wise idea that I needed to go back to being involved in coaching quarterbacks and calling plays. Managing everything. Pretending I was thirty-five again.

Truth is, when I'd *been* thirty-five, forty, when we were still raising a houseful of kids, I'd actually done a better job of maintaining a semblance of balance in my schedule. I made time for having breakfast with the family, for doing devotionals together, for taking the kids to school, and for getting to as many of their games and activities as I could possibly attend. I always found a way. Being with Katharyn and our family was a priority. But this time, at this age, while we still made sure to spend time together, neither one of us was as dependent on the other as our children had been. I could go a hundred miles an hour, knowing nobody was back there wondering when Dad was coming home.

So I could do it. I could put in the time that I hadn't been quite as free to give when I was still a father to four kids under one roof. I could coach; I could deal with player issues; I could work on the offensive game plan; I could lead the other guys on our staff; I could be out fund-raising for the indoor; I could even consult with Carlos Padron, superintendent of the indoor project, to be sure it had all the things we needed and wanted. And I enjoyed every bit of it. It was exhilarating. Compelling.

But it was a monster. It was eating me alive, and I didn't even know it. When you're a coach, you keep going. You think you can always just keep going.

Truth be told, I'd forgotten how important my quiet times were with God. I'd forgotten how much I needed that small group of couples that Katharyn and I once regularly met with to study the Bible and learn from each other, as well as my prayer group, my accountability group—the things I did at UGA that gave me the balance I needed for staying healthy, both mentally and spiritually. At Miami I did spend time once a week with our strength coach, Gus Felder, which was awesome, but I neglected the rest. Neglecting those things came back to bite me later.

We finished out 2017 with a really disheartening loss at Pitt, the last game of the season, ending our win streak at fifteen and putting a dagger in our championship hopes. But the year as a whole, even though it hadn't turned out to be every possible thing we could've dreamed of, was still a significant success. We won the Coastal division for the first time since joining the conference, and went to the Orange Bowl for the first time in thirteen years—an invitation that used to be practically automatic for Miami football.

And we picked up in 2018 exactly where we left off, predicted to win the Coastal division again and challenge for the ACC championship. We were preseason #8, ahead of everybody in our conference except for #2 Clemson, who'd lost the previous year to Alabama in the CFP semifinals. They would eventually go on to win it all in the 2018 season, their second title in three years.

But we intended to be in lockstep with them the whole way, rolling to a strong 5-1 record by the middle of October, our only loss coming to LSU in a neutral-site kickoff game at Arlington, Texas. Starting with game seven, though, we hit a downturn, dropping four in a row. First at Virginia, where the fans streamed out of that grassy end zone area again after the game, same as in '95. Then at Boston College, where a close game got away from us in the fourth quarter. We followed it up with a second-half collapse in the pouring rain at home against Duke, and then just didn't play well at Georgia Tech. Mistakes cost us. After starting well that day in Atlanta, we fumbled three times, twice on returns that they converted into points.

Disappointing.

The team kept battling, though. We righted the ship with two wins to close out the season, beating Pitt this time—a year too late—before finishing off with our third bowl in three years. *Okay,* I thought, *we can get this back together. We got this.*

Except that with the season ending and heavy recruiting coming up, suddenly none of the buttons you push to make your body bounce back and press ahead were working. I was simply exhausted. Not just exhausted but totally out of gas. No fire. Nothing left in the tank.

I had never felt so physically, mentally, and emotionally spent in my entire life. I thought I knew what fatigue felt like, but this . . . this was a level of fatigue I had never experienced. I was just worn slap out. And it was incredibly disturbing. Debilitating.

I'd been working too hard, too much, and I knew it. Not sleeping enough. Not eating right. Not exercising. But surely I could catch my breath and recharge. I *had* to. There wasn't any time to slow down. *Come on, Mark, let's go.*

But . . . nothing. I had nothing.

Thirty-five years. I'd been doing this for thirty-five years. The twelve-to-fourteen-hour days, seven days a week. The keeping everybody motivated. The building and maintaining of relationships. The constant searching for new talent. The constant responsibility for maximizing and maturing the talent you've already got.

Was it possible that I just couldn't do it anymore? What if I can't push past it? What if I literally can't talk myself out of bed in the morning? What's going to become of what we're building here?

While my body was on empty, my mind was busy torturing me with unsolvable, condemning trains of thought. On the one hand, I felt an almost all-absorbing duty to fulfill the expectations that I had for myself and for Miami. It was such an honor. It satisfied something deep and devoted in me. I also knew if I retired, it would create chaos for every coach and his family. Because when a new head coach gets hired, a new staff gets hired. In other words, everyone gets fired. Plus, it would mean leaving the players, which was the last thing I wanted to do. But on the other hand, if I stayed, I knew in my heart it would not be healthy for me, nor would it be in the best interest of the University of Miami. A hard pill to swallow, but true.

While my body was on empty, my mind was busy torturing me with unsolvable, condemning trains of thought.

So I did what I thought was in the best interest of everyone. I retired. One of the hardest things I've ever had to do in my career was to call every one of my coaches and tell them my decision. It was a bad day. They understood, but it was still a gut punch to them, because they knew what it meant for them: looking for new opportunities, putting houses up for sale, pulling their children out of schools, the whole works.

And to top it off, I made my decision during Christmas vacation, so all the players were out of town. I couldn't talk to them in person. My goal was to speak to them when they got back in town, which would be in only a couple of days. But by that time—much quicker than I expected—they'd already announced Manny Diaz as head coach. By the time the players returned, it was already Manny's team. So even though I think he would've allowed me to talk to them, I didn't want to interfere with the start of his tenure. All I could really do was shoot something out on social media. But I regret I couldn't speak with them first, to tell them myself, to give me a chance to explain it.

Have you ever had to make a call like that? You will, if you live long enough.

And I promise you, it won't be easy.

I mentioned earlier a verse that Christians like to use in helping them sort through tough decisions. "Let the peace of Christ rule in your hearts" (Col. 3:15). That's true. Trust Him to lead you to the kinds of choices and solutions that you can be at peace with. But don't think for one second that making hard calls, even for a Christian, is a peaceful experience. You may come to the point of knowing what you need to do, the way I came to it during this process, but don't expect to just follow your sense of peace and let it guide you through. The peace will be there eventually. Peace is there for me now. But there wasn't any peace to be found at the time.

It was such a hard call to make.

I left for my health and for Miami's well-being. That's it. I could've hung around, gone through the motions long enough until everybody else figured out what I already knew, that my physical ability to lead was diminishing. By then, after they'd fired me, my contract would've forced them to pay me millions of dollars not to work. Instead I walked out the door myself, leaving those millions behind.

> **Don't think for one second that making hard calls, even for a Christian, is a peaceful experience.**

But that's what you do when you know you're making the right call. It doesn't matter what it costs you. It doesn't matter the turmoil you feel, the questions that keep you up nights, the battling it takes to defuse all your doubts while you fight to believe. You didn't do what you did because it was easy. And yet somehow, by God's grace, you made it through.

The calls have to be made. Nobody can make them for you.

But you can make them . . . for all the right reasons.

EPILOGUE

Sudden Death

You've heard of going from zero to sixty. We went from sixty to zero.

Katharyn and I had found ourselves settled and happy in our new home on the Florida panhandle, overlooking the gentle surf coming in off the Gulf of Mexico. Most days started now with a morning walk, after which we'd head to the nearby gym for our individual workouts.

It was a Monday, October 21. Not even a year since I'd retired from my life as a head coach and become the talking-head voice of a former head coach on the ACC Network, a job I've really enjoyed. I was home from my weekend on-air duties, doing what I did every Monday morning now, trying to get my heart rate up. Trying to do a better job of keeping my body well.

There really wasn't much expertise to my old-man workout. I gravitated mostly to the lighter weights, doing higher reps, with not a lot of rest in between. The goal was to keep a little muscle mass and to get my heart pumping, to get the oxygen and blood flow going where it needed to go.

I'd made it to my last station that morning, a final round of military presses, alternating with a follow-up set of shrugs. Just morphing from one to the other and then back again. Military press, shrugs. Military press, shrugs. I was now on my third and last set of each one. Fifteen reps apiece. I was maybe on my eleventh or twelfth shrug, preparing to call it a day, when suddenly I just felt like I couldn't catch my breath.

I put the weight down, sweating hard, and just sat there trying to recover. I didn't know why I was feeling so unusually overheated. Maybe I'd just overdone it a little.

Then I felt a wave of nausea. That's when I thought I knew what it was. My wife and her silly vitamins. She liked us to take certain ones when we first got up, before we went for our walk and our workout, before we'd even had anything to eat. But I never really liked taking them on an empty stomach. I had a feeling that's what was bothering me now. If not that, I had no other explanation for it.

Still panting, I stood weakly to my feet and began working my way to the men's locker room. More specifically the bathroom. But even in trying to cool down, nothing was keeping me from continuing to get hotter. Just burning up. And still unable to get a good breath. Gosh. What did I need to do here?

I huffed over to one of the benches. I had just sat down, then laid down, flat of my back, laboring to breathe, when a scary thought flashed through my mind. *Was I having a heart attack?*

"Help!" I cried out. "I need help!"

Apparently no one was in the locker room. The only guy I'd seen in the few minutes that I'd been back there had apparently come in and left.

Shoot, if I don't get up, I might die here, I thought. The pain and pressure were really starting to build. I honestly didn't know if I could force myself to stand up. But you'll do what you've got to do when you're desperate. I've gone back in there in days since and counted the forty-five steps it took—out of the locker room, through the sauna and steam area, before finally reaching the door that led out into where all the workout equipment was. I staggered through it, went down to one knee, then to my butt, then to my back.

"I need help!" I cried again.

I thought for sure I was dying.

=====

Two EMTs from Sacred Heart Hospital in Miramar Beach—Wes Usher and Richie Frank—were about to go off their shift that morning, just as Luke Turner and Josh Pitts were coming on. So instead of having two guys show up in an ambulance, I got four when the call went out: "Chest pains, sweaty, shortness of breath."

Somebody had brought me some water to drink during the roughly ten minutes of waiting for the ambulance to arrive. I remember telling them, "Just throw it on me." All I wanted was to cool down. I didn't think I could stand it much longer.

That's the picture they got when they rushed into the gym, trying to assess my situation. As one of them wheeled in the gurney, I thought, *Just get me in the ambulance and give me some relief.* Once I was there, I thought maybe I'd be all right.

I wasn't all right.

They ran a quick EKG and confirmed, yes—I was having a heart attack. They called it in to the hospital as we sped down the road, sirens blasting, working desperately to start getting some saline flowing. But admittedly, I'm a hard stick. Gone were the days when the veins bulged rich and purple in my forearm. I could hear them cussing each failed attempt at stabbing the needle in, while my own struggles to breathe and cool down continued on, unabated.

Upon reaching the hospital, which thankfully was only a mile and a half away, they rolled me into the ER and quickly ran me through their triage process. Wes told me later that he was almost sure I was going to "code" (hospital slang for "die") right there in the emergency room. In fact, even as they wheeled me back to the cath lab, the attendants asked the EMTs to follow along, in case I went into cardiac arrest and needed to be resuscitated during the procedure.

But even with the extreme seriousness of the moment, even with the sense of urgency that I could feel all around me, I remember saying, "Wait, wait, wait! I've got to see my wife! I need to talk to Katharyn!"

She, of course, had been following the ambulance—had actually been driven by our friend Todd Thompson, a former high school coach who worked the front desk at the gym. They scrambled her into the hallway. She reached down and squeezed my hand.

I just told her I loved her, praying that I wasn't also telling her goodbye.

I was afraid I might not get another chance.

=====

Unbeknownst to me, when Katharyn got word through to our son Jon at his home about what was happening, he clicked off the line and fell to his knees, weeping. His young daughter— Jadyn's little sister, Zoe—seeing him distraught on the floor, ran over to her daddy, lay down next to him, and started singing "Jesus Loves Me."

=====

My blood pressure was dropping so precipitously in the operating room that they had to keep me awake instead of putting me all the way under. I was at too much risk. So while Dr. Mayes, the heart surgeon, worked to insert stents into *two* blocked arteries—both 100 percent blocked, including the left anterior descending artery [LAD], known as the "Widow Maker"—a female nurse sat near my head, repeatedly asking me, "How are you feeling? *What* are you feeling?"

I said, "My left arm feels numb. And I can't breathe."

A few moments later, she asked again. "What are you feeling?"

"Uh, it's my right arm now. Both arms feel numb."

Pretty soon it was my left leg. Then my right leg. It was like a creeping sense of numbness was just consuming my whole body, until finally I could feel it all the way up into my neck, into my jaw, into my face.

"What are you feeling?"

"My ears are going numb. And I can't breathe."

Whether I couldn't keep my eyes open or just didn't want to, I had kept them shut throughout the entire operation. Yet even with my eyes closed, the stark brightness of the lights in the room had been radiating through my eyelids the whole time. You know how that looks. But as the numbness overtook my head, all appearance of light slowly evaporated into darkness.

Everything went numb. Everything went dark. Pitch black.

I was thinking, *I'm shutting down. I'm dying. This is it.*

I don't want to characterize anything that happened next as being anything other than what it was. I won't say it was an out-of-body experience, but in my spirit I was calm, peaceful, even excited to go see Jesus, while at the same time my body was still battling to survive, still gasping for air.

I was dying, wasn't I? I was going to Jesus. I knew it in my spirit. And I was feeling strangely good. Happy even. I was . . .

Excited.

I'm serious.

I do remember thinking how much I was going to miss Katharyn. I remember that distinctly. But the overwhelming mood and reality that wrapped around me in that moment was a peace and joy and serenity at being ready. Ready to go to Jesus. A thankfulness for heaven. And an excitement. I was truly excited about what lay ahead.

And then . . .

"Wake up!"

That same steady, reassuring voice that earlier had been asking me how I was feeling was suddenly cutting through my calm head space, reminding me that my body was still fighting to live. I think she said something about, "He's got one stent in. He's working on the other"—because apparently, when Dr. Mayes got the Widow Maker open, and could tell I was still in pain, he looked and found the other artery that was blocked as well. That one required three stents. My heart episode had been that serious of an event.

But once all the passages were clear, once the blood started flowing again, that's my first memory of being able to inhale a deep, reviving breath of air.

Thank You, Lord. I said. To myself. Or to everybody. I don't know. *Thank You, Lord.* I could breathe again. I was going to make it.

Thank You, Lord.

—————

Obviously an experience like that will get your attention. I hope it's gotten yours. Because in the end, there's only one thing that's important.

What will happen to you when you come to that moment of truth, when there's no deal-making or last-minute cramming that can change the outcome of your eternal destiny? In the end, the only thing that matters is whether you've put your faith in Christ and received His forgiveness of all your sins, or whether you haven't.

Have you?

I'd always known, ever since feeling that wave of conviction in my heart after

> **In the end, the only thing that matters is whether you've put your faith in Christ and received His forgiveness of all your sins, or whether you haven't.**

Pablo Lopez's death and praying to receive Christ in Coach Bowden's office—I'd always known it was real. But we're human. We can't help having our doubts. And so, on those occasions, like, when an airplane would be rocking with turbulence, and I'd be trying to play it cool though my mind couldn't help realizing that airplanes really do crash and go down, I'd had that question pop into my mind. *Am I ready? Am I really ready?*

And while I don't recommend having a heart attack, I'm glad today that mine offered me the opportunity to confirm beyond any doubt in my mind that putting my faith in Christ was the right call. I don't know how many minutes or seconds away from death that I came that day, but I do know when I came face to face with the end of my life on Earth, I was ready for heaven. Christ had made me ready for heaven.

Christ can make you ready to face eternity.

Only Christ can do that.

By the time I got out of recovery and into a private room, family had already heard and were beginning to arrive from Georgia, from Tallahassee, from all around. I felt like I'd been beaten up, like my chest had been stomped on. I could breathe now, but I was sore.

"How are you feeling?" people would say. My main answer was, "I'm thankful." Thankful that I lived? Of course, yes. Thankful that I'd spotted the signs during the previous offseason, that I hadn't just pressed ahead and done the macho thing, putting myself and others in worse danger. But more than anything, I was thankful for my faith, and I was thankful that it was real. I was thankful that Jesus is real, like I knew He was. And thankful that I was His, like I knew I was, because of what He's done for me. Because of what He's done for all of us. Because of the cross. Because of His love.

─────

The 2006 Sugar Bowl was held in Atlanta instead of New Orleans that year because of the destruction suffered from Hurricane Katrina. Having won the SEC, we [Georgia] were back in a BCS bowl after defeating Florida State in the 2003 Sugar Bowl, 26–13.

Our opponent this time was West Virginia, who'd been climbing in stature under fifth-year coach Rich Rodriguez. Still, even though they'd put together a 10–1 season, we were favored by a touchdown. The game was ours to win.

But they jumped out to a *huge* first quarter lead. Every time they got the ball, they scored. With only a minute gone in the second, they were already up 28–0.

Finally we found some offense. And though the process had not been pretty, we somehow went into the locker room at halftime trailing by only ten, 31–21.

My speech to the guys was to tell them not to panic. "There's plenty of time, men. We just need to keep playing our game. We've got what it takes. Let's just go out there and do it. Plenty of time. Come on."

And we did. We went out and kept chipping. By the end of the third, we'd cut it down to a field goal. And though they busted us for a big touchdown run in the fourth, receiver Bryan McClendon, on the ensuing drive, put a wicked move on one of their defensive backs. Shockley found him wide open for a forty-three-yard bomb, and we were back in business again. Three points behind.

Roughly five minutes to go. All we needed was a defensive stop, and I knew—I knew!—we could pull off the comeback. "Plenty of time, guys. Plenty of time," I said, clapping and cheering them on from the sidelines.

At the two-minute mark, we'd held them. Fourth and six, the ball around midfield. They brought out their punt team, and I was already looking down at the call sheet, fired up. I'd seen by now what their defense could do. I knew exactly what we needed to run. We'd be facing a long field most likely, after the kick, but they hadn't been able to stop us in the last few series. Even if all we got was a field goal to tie it, I knew we'd be all right. *Let me just look this over, one more time,* I thought, as I scanned the play call sequence on my card.

With my mind already visualizing how we were going to win the game, I heard a roar echoing down from the pockets of West Virginia fans in the Georgia Dome. It was followed by an even louder moan, not only from the seats high above us but emanating from the players and coaches right around me.

Rich-Rod had called a fake punt.

The punter, after receiving the snap, ran the ball himself past the line to gain, down inside our 40, and slid to a stop with an unquestionable first down.

We never got the ball back.

There wasn't plenty of time after all. Time ran out.

It's hard to make a decision when you're dead, I've been known to say, after your time runs out. But there's time right now. There's time today. Time to give your heart to Jesus.

I wrote this book because I want to see you in heaven. Putting your faith in Jesus is the way to get there, through the forgiveness of your sins, making you right with God. We can't earn our way; we can't be good enough. We need a Savior, and His name is Jesus.

And so I ask you, just as Coach Bowden put the question to the team after the death of Pablo Lopez: if you had been the one who'd died last night instead of Pablo, do you know where you would spend eternity? It's time to make the call.

Time for *you* to make the call.

Acknowledgments

again want to thank my Lord and Savior Jesus Christ, for the blessings of a full life with Him. It's only because of what He's done to make me a new man, a new creation, that I've been able to navigate life and, as I now know for sure, be prepared for death. I'm still really excited about getting to see Him someday.

In addition to my wife, Katharyn, I also want to recognize the rest of our family with great love and gratitude: our son Jon and his wife, Anna, as well as their two children, our two granddaughters, Jadyn and Zoe; our son David and his wife, Joanna; our son Zach and our daughter Anya.

I'm grateful, too, for the home I grew up in and the people that God has continued to add to our family: my father, Lou, and my mother, Helen; my stepmother, Annette; my big brother, Lou; my younger brother, Craig, his wife, Jana, and their daughters Sammi, Aly, and Livi; my sister Mikki, her husband, Kevin, and their children, Elijah and Noelle; my baby sister Nikki, her husband, Brad, and their two sons, Max and Jake.

Along with giving me Katharyn, God has also blessed me with a whole other family to call my own: Katharyn's father, Bill, and her mother, Lynn; her stepmother, Elin; her brother Billy and his wife, Lisa, along with their children, Rowdy (including wife, Rachel, and son Finn), Evan, and Emma; Katharyn's sister Betsy, her husband, Brian, their daughters Whitney Lynn, Anne Elise, Karis, and Eden; also, Katharyn's brother Bobby, his wife, Tricia, and their daughters, Trinity and Ramsey.

In the end, the two most important things are God and family!

A close third, for me, would be my players. I've had the honor of recruiting and coaching hundreds of players in my career, and nearly each one of them brings to mind another story that I wish

I could've included in this book. I couldn't squeeze them all in, but I hope you know how much you and your families mean to me.

Certainly when I think of my players, it brings to mind the respect I feel for all the coaches I've ever worked with or worked under, starting with Coach Bowden, but including many, many more—not just coaches, but also support staff. Your professionalism and love for our players helped make them better men, and me a better man. If it's true that the reason any of us started playing football at all was mainly so we could be with our friends, God has truly given me a lot of great friends over the years to coach ball with. Those friends would also include the many administrators, fans, boosters, and former teammates who've been instrumental in enabling me to play and coach the game I love.

I want to thank my literary agent, D. J. Snell, for representing me on this, my first book. (I've enjoyed it more than I expected. I hope it won't be the last.) Thanks also to sports journalist Jeff Snook, especially for his recollection and confirmation of events surrounding the Pablo Lopez story.

Finally, thanks to the team at Lifeway and at B&H Publishing in Nashville: Devin Maddox; editors Taylor Combs and Kim Stanford; marketing pros Mary Wiley and Jenaye White; art designers Susan Browne and Jade Novak, and all the others who work so hard to put messages like mine into the hands of people like you, who will hopefully be impacted by them. Special thanks go to my new friend Lawrence Kimbrough for helping me collect all these stories into a form that made them easy to follow and fun to share, and for capturing the intent of my heart in print.

As I said before, my greatest prayer, now that you've read this book, is that it's drawn you to Jesus, either for the first time or maybe for the first time in a long time. Don't let His desire to seek you out through these pages go to waste. Let's meet up in heaven, you and me, where we can be excited about seeing Him together.

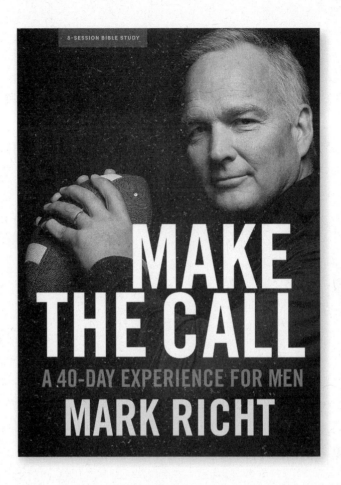

APPLY THE WISDOM IN THIS BOOK TO YOUR EVERYDAY ROUTINE

Use this 40-day playbook to equip yourself or your men's group to make godly decisions and clarify what's most important in life.

- Each day features a Scripture, a short devotional, and reflective questions.
- This resource includes guides for an eight-session small group experience.

lifeway.com/makethecall